1505

105819

S13

34

RICH is NOT a bad word

DR. MICHAEL D. MOORE

MIKE MOORE MINISTRIES

"Rich" Is Not a Bad Word
Discover the Keys to Unlock the Blessing of God's Abundance into Your Life
ISBN 0-96784-392-8
Copyright © 2007 by Dr. Michael D. Moore

Published by Mike Moore Ministries
800 Quebec Drive
Birmingham, Alabama 35224

Acknowledgments

Kennetha Moore:
My wife and very best friend for your support,
faith, and confidence in me during this project.

Michael and Tiffany Moore:
The best children a father could ever hope to have.

Andrea Spencer:
For all your support in putting this book together.

Faith Chapel Christian Center:
The most loving church in all the world!

Contents

Introduction

*The blessing of the Lord makes one rich,
and He adds no sorrow with it.*
Proverbs 10:22

Because such stories as the rich young ruler in Mark 10 and the rich man in Luke 12 have not been correctly understood, many people have been deceived into thinking that there is something wrong with being rich. All of us have heard 1 Timothy 6:10 misquoted as "money is the root of all evil" when the Scripture clearly says, *the love of money is a root of all kinds of evil*. . . .

Many also misinterpret verse 17: *Command those who are rich in this present age not to be haughty, nor to trust in uncertain riches but in the living God, who gives us richly all things to enjoy.* They read it as an admonition not to have wealth, while God is merely telling us not to let riches affect our attitude in the wrong way.

In this powerful teaching, Dr. Michael D. Moore corrects misunderstandings, imparts new revelation, and reassures us that being rich is not bad and that "rich" is not a bad word. In fact, he illustrates conclusively that God is in the business of making His people rich, not poor. God wants us to have abundance — an overflow of wealth. That overflow will allow us to give generously to the Kingdom. Riches are only a problem for those who do not fully understand that it is God's greatest desire to abundantly bless His children.

—THE EDITORS

1
CHAPTER

Wealth Without Sorrow

The blessing of the Lord makes one rich,
and He adds no sorrow with it.
Proverbs 10:22

Much of what Christians call "being blessed" is really not the blessing of the Lord because in reality there is too much sorrow associated with it. You don't have to sacrifice your relationship with God or with your family, your integrity, your health, or even your commitment to your local church to get wealth. The Bible says that when God blesses us, there won't be any sorrow added to it.

God will not give you a job that takes you away from your family and your church. A lot of Christians who think that they are following the Lord are actually being led by money. They accept a job that takes time away from their spouse, children, and church and mistakenly think they are doing God's will. God never gives you a house that triggers stress as a result of having to pay an outlandish mortgage, or "blesses" you with a car payment so high that you can't tithe. You tithed before you got the house and before you got the car. But, because of the "blessing" God "gave you," now you can't tithe anymore because you have to pay your mortgage. You can't give anymore because you have to pay your car note. Such things are clearly not the blessing of the Lord.

The blessing of the Lord brings wealth, and no sorrow comes with it. This verse implies that some wealth is accompanied by sorrow. That kind of wealth occurs when you gain it on your own without regard to God's will.

Many Christians don't realize that God wants them blessed and prosperous. If we can find people in the Bible whom God made rich, then the word "rich" must not be a bad word.

Let's look briefly at the lives of Abram (who became Abraham), Isaac, Jacob, Joseph, David, Solomon, Job, and Joseph of Arimathea. These men were each very wealthy.

ABRAM

Look at Genesis 13:2:

Abram was very rich in livestock, in silver, and in gold.

This verse is not referring to "spiritual" wealth. Cattle, silver, and gold are not metaphors for some spiritual attributes that Abram possessed. He was rich in material possessions.

Let's follow Abram, or Abraham, through Genesis 14:20-23:

"And blessed be God Most High, who has delivered your enemies into your hand." And he gave him a tithe of all. Now the king of Sodom said to Abram, "Give me the persons, and take the goods for yourself." But Abram said to the king of Sodom, "I have raised my hand to the Lord, God Most High, the Possessor of heaven and earth, that I will take nothing, from a thread to a sandal strap, and that I will not take anything that is yours, lest you should say, 'I have made Abram rich.'"

Abram turned his back on man. Essentially, he was saying, "Man will not be my source. I will not look to a job, nor will I look to anything in this earth. No man will ever be able to say he made me rich. God is going to be my source."

Now notice God's response in Genesis 15:1:

After these things the word of the Lord came to Abram in a vision, saying, "Do not be afraid, Abram. I am your shield, your exceedingly great reward."

Abram looked to God, not man. And God said, "I like that! I am your protector, and I am your exceedingly great reward."

Abram's servant confirms God's graciousness to him in Genesis 24:35:

"The Lord has blessed my master greatly, and he has become great; and He has given him flocks and herds, silver and gold, male and female servants, and camels and donkeys."

So, who blessed Abram? The Lord did.

ISAAC

Look at Isaac in Genesis 26:12-14:

Then Isaac sowed in that land, and reaped in the same year a hundredfold; and the Lord blessed him. The man began to prosper, and continued prospering until he became very prosperous; for he had possessions of flocks and possessions of herds and a great number of servants. So the Philistines envied him.

Who blessed Isaac? God blessed him.

JACOB

Let's now examine the life of Jacob in Genesis 30:43:

Thus the man became exceedingly prosperous, and had large flocks, female and male servants, and camels and donkeys.

It looks as if Jacob was rich. In Genesis 32:9-10 we find Jacob's own testimony:

Then Jacob said, "O God of my father Abraham and God of my father Isaac, the Lord who said to me, 'Return to your country and to your family, and I will deal well with you': I am not worthy of the least of all the mercies and of all the truth which You have shown Your servant; for I crossed over this Jordan with my staff, and now I have become two companies. . . ."

Here Jacob is letting us know that when he left home, he did not have anything. He was penniless. Notice, Jacob credits God for his wealthy state.

This is what Jacob says in Genesis 33:11 when he comes face-to-face with his brother Esau:

"Please, take my blessing that is brought to you, because God has dealt graciously with me, and because I have enough."

So, who blessed Jacob? God blessed him.

JOSEPH

Now let's look at Joseph in Genesis 39:1-2:

Now Joseph had been taken down to Egypt. And Potiphar, an officer of Pharaoh, captain of the guard, an Egyptian, bought him from the Ishmaelites who had taken him down there. The

Lord was with Joseph, and he was a successful man. . . .

In chapter 41 we see just how much Joseph prospered because the Lord was with him.

Then Pharaoh said to Joseph, "Inasmuch as God has shown you all this, there is no one as discerning and wise as you. You shall be over my house, and all my people shall be ruled according to your word; only in regard to the throne will I be greater than you." And Pharaoh said to Joseph, "See, I have set you over all the land of Egypt." Then Pharaoh took his signet ring off his hand and put it on Joseph's hand; and he clothed him in garments of fine linen and put a gold chain around his neck. And he had him ride in the second chariot which he had; and they cried out before him, "Bow the knee!" So he set him over all the land of Egypt.

Genesis 41:39-43

Joseph came out of slavery and became a very powerful and wealthy man. Who blessed Joseph?

Look at verses 51-52. The Bible says that Joseph had two sons in Egypt.

Joseph called the name of the firstborn Manasseh: "For God has made me forget all my toil and all my father's house." And the name of the second he

*called Ephraim: "For God has caused me to be fruit-
ful in the land of my affliction."*

Truly, it was God who blessed Joseph.

DAVID

Now let's look at David. You have to get a revelation
that the word "rich" is not a bad word. *God wants to
bless you, but He can't if you have erroneous thoughts
concerning wealth. Also, He can't prosper you if you
are satisfied with your present financial status.* Some
people are content with simply having their needs met,
but that's not being rich. It's not God's plan for you to
just be able to pay your bills. Life is bigger than that.

Look at 1 Chronicles 29:28:

*So he [David] died in a good old age, full of days
and riches and honor. . . .*

That's what God wants for you. He wants you to live a
long and prosperous life.

We know that God blessed David because he identifies
the source of his wealth in 1 Chronicles 29:10-14:

*Therefore David blessed the Lord before all the
assembly; and David said: "Blessed are You, Lord
God of Israel, our Father, forever and ever. Yours,
O Lord, is the greatness, the power and the glory,
the victory and the majesty; for all that is in heaven
and in earth is Yours; Yours is the kingdom, O*

Lord, and You are exalted as head over all. Both riches and honor come from You, and You reign over all. In Your hand is power and might; in Your hand it is to make great and to give strength to all. Now therefore, our God, we thank You and praise Your glorious name. But who am I, and who are my people, that we should be able to offer so willingly as this? For all things come from You, and of Your own we have given You. . . ."

Who made David rich? God did!

SOLOMON

Let's look at Solomon in 2 Chronicles 1:7:

On that night God appeared to Solomon, and said to him, "Ask! What shall I give you?"

What if God appeared to you and said, "Ask Me for whatever you want"? What would you say in response? Your answer is the key to what God will do, as we see in 2 Chronicles 1:8-12:

And Solomon said to God, "You have shown great mercy to David my father, and have made me king in his place. Now, O Lord God, let Your promise to David my father be established, for You have made me king over a people like the dust of the earth in multitude. Now give me wisdom and knowledge, that I may go out and come in before this people; for who can judge this great people of Yours?" Then

God said to Solomon: "Because this was in your heart, and you have not asked riches or wealth or honor or the life of your enemies, nor have you asked long life — but have asked wisdom and knowledge for yourself, that you may judge My people over whom I have made you king — wisdom and knowledge are granted to you; and I will give you riches and wealth and honor, such as none of the kings have had who were before you, nor shall any after you have the like."

Who made Solomon rich? God did!

JOB

Next, let's look at Job 1:1-3:

There was a man in the land of Uz, whose name was Job; and that man was blameless and upright, and one who feared God and shunned evil. And seven sons and three daughters were born to him. Also, his possessions were seven thousand sheep, three thousand camels, five hundred yoke of oxen, five hundred female donkeys, and a very large household, so that this man was the greatest of all the people of the East.

Who blessed Job and made him rich? Even the devil testifies of God's goodness. Notice what the devil says to God:

God has
no favorites.

"Have You not made a hedge around him, around his household, and around all that he has on every side? You have blessed the work of his hands, and his possessions have increased in the land."

Job 1:10

Even the devil acknowledges that God blessed Job. In chapter 42, the Bible says the Lord turned the captivity of Job and gave him twice as much as he had before.

The Lord blessed Job with many riches, not the devil.

JOSEPH OF ARIMATHEA

It takes money to get the Gospel of Jesus Christ preached and to get people saved.

In Matthew 27:57-60 we find an example of the difference a rich person can make in furthering the Gospel of Jesus Christ:

Now when evening had come, there came a rich man from Arimathea, named Joseph, who himself had also become a disciple of Jesus. This man went to Pilate and asked for the body of Jesus. Then Pilate commanded the body to be given him. When Joseph had taken the body, he wrapped it in a clean linen cloth, and laid it in his new tomb which he had hewn out of the rock; and he rolled a large stone against the door of the tomb, and departed.

Notice in these verses that you can be a disciple and be rich at the same time. You don't have to be poor to follow Jesus. Because of Joseph's notable economic status and position in the community, he was able to gain an audience with — and subsequently influence — Pilate. However, Pilate would not have listened to a poor person. (Ecclesiastes 9:16.)

Look at Acts 10:34:

Then Peter opened his mouth and said: "In truth I perceive that God shows no partiality."

This means "He is no accepter of a face." In other words, He does not embrace one face above another. The Bible tells us that God has no favorites. He shows no partiality. What He will do for one, He will do for another. If we can find one man in Scripture whom God made rich, then we have a right to believe for the same thing. Actually, we found eight examples of such men!

In Acts 10:35 we read:

But in every nation [The word "nation" is the Greek word *ethnos,* and it means race of men. It means that skin color does not matter to God.] *whoever fears Him* [You've got to respect God and His ways.] *and works righteousness is accepted by Him.*

What's being discussed here is not positional righteousness or just being saved. It's practical righteousness — doing what is right in God's sight.

REVIEW OF THE LIFE PRINCIPLES OF THESE EIGHT MEN

Let's look again at the eight people I referred to previously and examine their lives to identify some of the life principles by which they lived:

1. Abraham

Abraham was a man of faith, so you've got to be a person of faith, as well. Also, Abraham was a tither, and he followed God's plan for his life.

2. Isaac

Isaac was a giver. He sowed and received, even in a time of famine. In other words, he continued to sow in the hard times. So don't just wait until things get better. Start to give *now* regardless of your present circumstances. Tithe in complete trust, a trust anchored in God, and He will bless you.

3. Jacob

Jacob went from transition to tribulation to transformation. He started out as a liar, a cheat, and a thief. Jacob lacked integrity and God couldn't bless him. That's why he left home penniless.

If you lack integrity, if you are a liar, a cheat, a manipulator, or a con artist, or if you continually take advantage of people, God can't bless you. The life of Jacob reveals that the Word will not work in a dishonest heart.

4. Joseph

Joseph exemplified the power of vision and forgiveness. He came to Egypt as a slave. Many disadvantages surrounded him: He was a member of a minority group. He was uneducated and inexperienced in the customs and culture of Egypt. He lacked sociopolitical influence, didn't know anyone, and had no friends or material resources. In spite of all this, God elevated him.

You are a *steward* of what God gives you.

Joseph teaches us that God is not limited by our limitations. However, He is limited by our faith and by our vision. What is vision? It is the ability to see beyond what is at the present time. Joseph was a man of vision. What would you do if God elevated you to such a position of power after your brothers had sold you into slavery? What would you do if Potiphar's wife lied about you and caused you to be imprisoned, but you ultimately found yourself in such a powerful position? What would you do? Joseph's response was to forgive his offenders and bless them.

5. David

David's example shows the importance of stewardship. David said that everything he possessed came from God. He could give freely because he didn't think he owned anything. Unlike David, most people think they are owners, but they aren't. They think they own the house they live in, but they don't. They think they own the car they drive, but they don't. They think they own the money they have in the bank, but they don't. The fact is, they don't own anything. When they go to the grave, what do they take with them? You must remember that you don't own anything. You are simply a *steward* of what God gives you. This is what David's life reveals.

6. Solomon

Solomon's life teaches us about right priorities — the importance of having your heart and motives in the right place and order. Don't pursue things; pursue God. You've got to love God and His people. Solomon placed God over himself. When he could have asked for houses and land, he didn't. Instead, he said, "Lord, give me wisdom."

7. Job

Job exemplified the importance of patience — never giving up, never quitting. Some people think God took everything from Job, but He didn't take anything. The Bible says that it was the devil who took those things from him. John 10:10 tells us that the thief comes to steal, kill, and destroy. Likewise, 1 Peter 5:8 says, *Be sober, be vigilant; because your adversary the devil walks about like a roaring lion, seeking whom he may devour.*

Someone might ask, "Well, didn't God allow the devil to steal from Job?" Of course He *allowed* it to happen. He will allow anything to happen *that you allow*. Job 1:5

teaches us that the immorality of Job's children gave Satan license to operate in their lives. The Bible says in Job 3:25-26 that Job's fear is what gave the devil a license to operate in his life.

8. Joseph of Arimathea

Joseph of Arimathea was a rich man who had influence. The Bible says that he went to see Pilate. Not just anyone can request audience with a political leader and have it granted to them. There are some places you can't go if you don't have money, position, or influence. There are some assignments that God can only give to prosperous people. For example, there are people who strictly fly first class whom God wants to reach, but He can't use you to minister to these people if you are flying in coach. It isn't a bad thing to fly coach; this is just an example of the opportunities God could open up to you if you have financial blessing in your life.

We also learn from Joseph of Arimathea that he was willing to share his wealth and possessions. He was available and what he had was available. The Bible says he gave his new tomb for Jesus' burial. He had purchased the tomb for himself, but Jesus had a need and Joseph was willing to meet that need. That's why God could trust him with money.

2
CHAPTER

Be Aware of the Cautions

*If riches increase, do not set
your heart on them.*
Psalm 62:10

When it comes to material wealth — finances, money, riches — there are cautions sprinkled throughout the Old and New Testaments because anything that has power can be either beneficial or detrimental. When riches are mishandled, misused, or misappropriated, they can be destructive.

The Word gives many cautions or warnings concerning riches. To be cautious means to be circumspect, to look around, to consider all the circumstances and consequences, always watching for danger. Drivers practice caution when they see flashing yellow signals. These signals prompt us to slow down, to proceed with care, and to be watchful for pedestrians and traffic.

But cautions are not stop signals, and we don't want to stop when we approach them. They are not detours either; we don't want to get off our intended course. We simply need to proceed carefully. The mistake we often make in Christianity is getting into a mindset thinking that God says material things are wrong, and then concluding we must avoid prosperity. This is not the case. God merely gives us cautions regarding wealth.

CAUTION #1

Here is the first caution: ***Don't forget God!*** One danger associated with increase of any kind is the temptation to forget God. A good proof text for this truth can be found in Deuteronomy 8:11-14,17-18:

> *"Beware that you do not forget the Lord your God by not keeping His commandments, His judgments, and His statutes which I command you today, lest — when you have eaten and are full, and have built beautiful houses and dwell in them; and when your herds and your flocks multiply, and your silver and your gold are multiplied, and all that you have is multiplied; when your heart is lifted up, and you forget the Lord your God who brought you out of the land of Egypt, from the house of bondage . . . then you say in your heart, 'My power and the might of my hand have gained me this wealth.' And you shall remember the Lord your God, for it is He who gives you power to get wealth, that He may establish His covenant which He swore to your fathers, as it is this day."*

Notice that this passage says it's when you are full that you may be tempted. You don't forget God when you struggle. In tribulation you tend to have a strong prayer life, and God stands foremost in your mind. He says it is when you are living in abundance — when you're living in a nice house or when your income starts increasing — that it is easy to fall into the trap of thinking your education and hard work got you to that place. God says, "No, no! Don't forget Me."

Let's take another look at Solomon in 1 Kings 11:1,3-4,6-8:

But King Solomon loved many foreign women, as well as the daughter of Pharaoh: women of the Moabites, Ammonites, Edomites, Sidonians, and Hittites . . . And he had seven hundred wives, princesses, and three hundred concubines; and his wives turned away his heart. For it was so, when Solomon was old, that his wives turned his heart after other gods; and his heart was not loyal to the Lord his God, as was the heart of his father David . . . Solomon did evil in the sight of the Lord, and did not fully follow the Lord, as did his father David. Then Solomon built a high place for Chemosh the abomination of Moab, on the hill that is east of Jerusalem, and for Molech the abomination of the people of Ammon. And he did likewise for all his foreign wives, who burned incense and sacrificed to their gods.

When Solomon was young and inexperienced, his heart sought after and yearned for the things of God. He said, "Give me wisdom and knowledge," and the Lord answered, "Because that was in your heart, not only will I give you wisdom and knowledge, but I am going to give you riches like no other king." But guess what? Solomon forgot God. That's the first warning or caution: *Don't forget God.*

How will you know when you have forgotten God? When you are no longer mindful of Him or His Word, your desire to obey Him has waned, and you become caught up in your financial position, prestige, and status.

When these things happen, it is obvious that you've forgotten God.

CAUTION #2

Here is the second caution: ***Don't put your trust in material wealth!*** There is a great proof text for this admonition. It is found in Psalm 62:10:

If riches increase, do not set your heart on them.

As riches increase in your life, you may experience a strong temptation to transfer your trust from the Giver to the gift. We have a good example of this in Mark 10:17-25. The rich young ruler prospered because he had observed all the biblical commandments since his youth in accordance with Deuteronomy 28:1-14.

However, in Mark 10:20-25, notice the shift in his trust:

And he answered and said to Him, "Teacher, all these things I have kept from my youth." Then Jesus, looking at him, loved him, and said to him, "One thing you lack [Just one thing? What if the Lord said something like that to you? You'd probably feel you were in pretty good shape if you were lacking just one thing.]: *Go your way, sell whatever you have and give to the poor, and you will have treasure in heaven; and come, take up the cross, and follow Me." But he was sad at this word, and went away sorrowful, for he had great possessions. Then Jesus looked around and said to His disciples, "How hard it is for those who have riches to enter the kingdom of God!" And the disciples were astonished at His words. But Jesus answered again and said to them, "Children, how hard it is for those who trust* [Oh, the issue is trust, not the riches!] *in riches to enter the kingdom of God! It is easier for a camel to go through the eye of a needle than for a rich man to enter the kingdom of God."*

Trust comes easily when you don't have anything. If you take a poor, struggling man and share with him the transforming Word of God, it is very probable that he will turn his heart and trust toward God. However, it's more difficult to stay mindful of God when you have material wealth.

When you struggle to make ends meet, you get "in God's face," and He causes increase to come because you are seeking Him and His will. But when increase comes, if you are not careful, you will respond just like that rich young ruler.

How do you know when you are placing your trust in material things? Here's the answer: You know that you trust in material things when God can't instruct you concerning their use. If it's difficult for you to give or sow into the lives of others, that difficulty may be caused by your misplaced value and trust in your possessions. That is why some people in church literally grieve around offering time. Sometimes they even go into mourning! They put their offering in the bucket, and they watch the bucket go all the way down the aisle. Why? They perceive giving as a loss. They're grieving because they have unknowingly turned their confidence and trust away from God's ability and instead turned their focus toward things.

CAUTION #3

The third caution is this: ***Don't live a selfish lifestyle!*** There's nothing worse than a selfish Christian. Christians are redeemed people who were headed to hell and saved by the ultimate love of Jesus. Out of sheer gratefulness for God's gift of eternal life to us, Christians should be anything but selfish. The proof text for this is found in Philippians 2, where we are told to stop looking at our interests only and practice looking out for the interests of others. (Philippians 2:4.)

Let's now look at a related example in Luke 12:16-19:

Then he spoke a parable to them, saying: "The ground of a certain rich man yielded plentifully. [Now count the times he says "I" and "my."] *And he thought within himself, saying, 'What shall I do, since I have no room to store my crops?' So he said, 'I will do this: I will pull down my barns and build greater, and there I will store all my crops and my goods. And I will say to my soul, "Soul, you have many goods laid up for many years; take your ease; eat, drink, and be merry.""*

Notice, he said "I" six times and "my" five times, which gives us an indication of what happened. He forgot why God blessed him. Do you know why God blesses you with more than you need? It's not to stack it up for yourself, but to help others and be a blessing. So, how can you know when you are living a selfish lifestyle? You will

A truly abundant life comes out of a meaningful relationship with God.

know you are living a selfish lifestyle when too many "I's" and "my's" fill your conversation and your life.

CAUTION #4

Luke 12 also offers us a fourth warning: ***Don't be a fool!*** Remember, these are not stop signals, just warnings or cautions.

Luke 12:19-21 states:

"'And I will say to my soul, "Soul, you have many goods laid up for many years; take your ease; eat, drink, and be merry."' But God said to him, 'Fool! [It's one thing when people call you a fool. You can kind of shake it off because they may or may not be right. But if God calls you a fool . . . .] *This night your soul will be required of you; then whose will those things be which you have provided?' So is*

he who lays up treasure for himself, and is not rich toward God."

So, don't be a fool. Proverbs 1:32 says, *And the complacency of fools will destroy them.* Why was the man in Luke 12 a fool? Because of the riches he possessed? No, God called him a fool because he thought his life was a result of the material resources he acquired. He thought the more he acquired, the more life he would have. That's why he said to his soul, "You have much goods laid up for many years" — much goods, many years. He thought that life came out of things. He was a fool because he was unable to comprehend that life is far more than having things. A truly abundant life comes out of a meaningful relationship with God. You will never get life from material possessions.

God wants you to enjoy every good gift in life, but remove God from the mix and you'll be in misery. In fact, Jesus says in Luke 12:15:

"Take heed and beware of covetousness, for one's life does not consist in the abundance of the things he possesses."

In other words, even when a man has more than enough, his wealth does not give him fulfillment in life. It is possible to have an abundance of things and still be lonely. It is possible to have an abundance of material wealth and still be sick, suicidal, miserable, and even die a premature death. You can't get life out of possessions. Abundant life comes from God, and you can only truly enjoy material possessions when you have a healthy relationship with God.

God wants you to have a blessed life, and that is why He doesn't want you to be foolish. That's why He has given these warnings and cautions in the Bible. If the sign says "slow down," you should slow down. Remember, these cautions are for our benefit.

CAUTION #5

The fifth caution is this: ***Don't become arrogant!*** Now what does it mean to be arrogant? "Arrogance" is a feeling of superiority, an exaggerated opinion of yourself, your worth, or your importance. It's thinking you are better than others. Here is a proof text about arrogance in 1 Timothy 6:17:

Command those who are rich in this present age not to be haughty. . . .

There are three things you should know about haughty [or arrogant] people:

One: ***They look down on others.*** They are generally egotistical and have become overconfident. However, God is in love with people — black, white, red, yellow, and brown people; rich, poor, educated, and uneducated people — as He sees their potential.

Two: ***They exclude and reject people they regard as being beneath or different from them.*** The church cannot be exclusive; it has to include everyone.

The value of a family can never be replaced.

People should be able to come into the church family and feel complete acceptance and a sense of belonging. That is how God intended it to be.

Three: *They don't love people; they use people.* To them, people are a means to an end. To God, we are all valuable and play an integral part in His plan.

CAUTION #6

Now let's look at the sixth caution or warning: *Don't be deceived by riches and neglect your spiritual life!* The two go together. If you place all of your trust in your riches, then you will not see the significance of maintaining a strong spiritual life.

The proof text for this warning is found in Mark 4:19:

"And the cares of this world, the deceitfulness of riches, and the desires for other things entering in choke the word, and it becomes unfruitful."

Jesus talks about the deceitfulness of riches. Isn't that a strange way to put it — the deceitfulness of riches? The word "deceitful" has two definitions. One of its meanings is delusion. A "delusion" involves a misleading of the mind or a misleading in judgment. The second definition is false appearance, something that appears to be or to offer one thing but actually produces a false sense of security.

That's the thing about finances and money: If you are not careful, your life can lose focus and get out of balance. It is during these times that you develop a false sense of security. You can fall into the trap of looking to possessions as a sense of guarantee. I see this happening to people all the time, even in the church. I've seen Christians take jobs and move to cities before they locate a church. They don't even think about looking for a church until they get there. They examine the school system and the neighborhood, but they don't think about a church home. Likewise, I've seen people accept jobs that take them away from their homelife. They were spending time with their families but then took a particular job that paid more money. And they find themselves traveling alone without time to share with their spouse or children. That's a dangerous deception.

Be willing to discipline yourself to put your spiritual life first.

You may not realize this, but on your deathbed, you are not going to talk about how much overtime you worked. As you get older, relationships will become more important to you. This point is particularly important for men. If you work long hours and neglect spending time with your family, when your children grow up they won't even know you. If you allow it, money will actually rob you; it will deceive you into thinking that its pursuit should be your top priority. What really matters is the quality of your relationships. The value of a family can never be replaced.

I want to show you a man in Luke 16:19-31 who was deceived by riches and neglected his spiritual life:

"There was a certain rich man who was clothed in purple and fine linen and fared sumptuously every day. But there was a certain beggar named Lazarus, full of sores, who was laid at his gate, desiring to be fed with the crumbs which fell from the rich man's table. Moreover the dogs came and licked his sores. So it was that the beggar died, and was carried by the angels to Abraham's bosom. The rich man also died and was buried. And being in torments in Hades, he lifted up his eyes and saw Abraham afar off, and Lazarus in his bosom. Then he cried and said, 'Father Abraham, have mercy on me, and send Lazarus that he may dip the tip of his finger in water and cool my tongue; for I am tormented in this flame.' But Abraham said, 'Son, remember that in your lifetime you received your good things, and likewise Lazarus evil things; but now he is comforted and you are tormented. And besides all this, between us and you there is a great gulf fixed, so that those who want to pass from here to you cannot, nor can those from there pass to us.' Then he said, 'I beg you therefore, father, that you would send him to my father's house, for I have five brothers, that he may testify to them, lest they also come to this place of torment.' Abraham said to him, 'They have Moses and the prophets; let them hear them.' And he said, 'No, father Abraham; but if one goes to them from the dead, they will repent.'

But he said to him, 'If they do not hear Moses and the prophets, neither will they be persuaded though one rise from the dead.'"

How did this rich man end up in hell? Did he go to hell because he was rich? No. (Do you go to heaven because you are poor? No.) He went to hell because riches deceived him, and he neglected his spiritual life. He was selfish and didn't have time for spiritual things. Many people like him are headed for the same destination. They don't spend much time reading the Bible or praying. Do you know why? Because they are too busy. Some people are so occupied with acquiring what God wants to give them that they neglect their spiritual life. That is deception.

God watches us as we go through the various stages of our lives. When my ministry was in its infancy, no one was coming to the church, and I had plenty of time to study, pray, and develop certain disciplines. Now, as the church has grown and prospered, I still have those disciplines because I established them in lean times. The reason God can't bless some people is because they don't have discipline. You must be willing to discipline yourself to put your spiritual life first.

3
CHAPTER

Keeping Your Balance

*"But seek first the kingdom of God and
His righteousness, and all these things
shall be added to you."*
Matthew 6:33

I remember when I was a boy and my parents bought me a bike with training wheels. When I first started riding my bike I didn't know how to balance myself very well, so I would usually lean to the left or to the right. The training wheels helped hold me up until I learned how to balance myself. That's what the first three chapters of this book are all about. They are designed to keep you balanced, to help you stay in the middle of the road, and to keep you from falling.

God has four concerns: (1) your priorities, (2) your motives, (3) your attitude, and (4) where you place your trust. These four areas are "the training wheels" that will keep you spiritually balanced.

FINANCIAL PRIORITY

Here is God's first concern: **What is your financial priority?**

Let's look at Matthew 6:32-33.

"For after all these things [Jesus has been teaching about material things: housing, clothing, etc.] *the Gentiles seek. For your heavenly Father knows that you need all these things. But seek first the kingdom of God and His righteousness, and all these things shall be added to you."*

God knows that you live in a material world and that you have material needs, but He says, *Seek first. . . .* (Now the word "first" implies that there is a second. A first without a second is an "only." You wouldn't say "my firstborn child" if you had only one child.) *But seek first the kingdom of God. . . .* The Kingdom of God is God's way of doing things.

Matthew 6:33 is probably one of the most misunderstood verses in the Bible. Most Christians don't even know what it means to seek first the Kingdom of God. Many think He's talking about getting saved, but this is not the case.

I have four observations concerning the word "first":

Observation 1: **When you place acquiring material things ahead of God, family, and church, your priorities are out of God's order.**

Observation 2: *Your financial priorities are proven, or demonstrated, by how you invest your money or other financial resources.* I can tell what your priorities are, regardless of what you say, by looking at either your budget or a record of your spending. The two are not the same. A budget is a plan of how you intend to spend your money. A record of your spending is how you have actually spent your money. I can look at either one and tell what your financial priorities are.

If you want to know what a man's heart is like, trace his money.

What does seeking first the Kingdom of God involve? Jesus answers this question in Matthew 6:19-21:

"Do not lay up for yourselves treasures on earth, where moth and rust destroy and where thieves break in and steal; but lay up for yourselves treasures in heaven, where neither moth nor rust destroys and where thieves do not break in and steal. For where your treasure is, there your heart will be also."

God never says it's wrong to have a checking or savings account. Nor is He saying it's wrong to invest in mutual funds or CDs. He is, however, talking about your priorities. He asks, "What do you put first?" He talks about investing in the Kingdom, using your finances for His work in the earth. He says, *Where your treasure is, there your heart will be also.* In other words, "Show me the money."

What you really love, you will invest in. That's the bottom line. Notice that He doesn't ask about your time. Nor does He ask about your talent or your service. These are important, to be sure, and you should give your time, talent, and service to God. Notice that He does not say anything about church membership here, or even about attending church faithfully. It's possible to attend church faithfully, to serve in the church, and still not seek God first. Jesus says if you want to know what a man's heart is like, trace his money. People will give God their time and service, but when you start to talk about money, it's an entirely different matter.

Observation 3: *Is the establishment of God's works in the earth a financial priority with you?* When you receive income, do you think, *I'll invest in the Kingdom and use the money to further God's work,* or do you think first about yourself? Is your financial priority arranged like this: you first, then God?

Observation 4: *It is impossible to seek first the Kingdom of God without being a tither and a giver, and you can't be a giver unless you are a tither first.* To tithe is to bring God 10 percent of all legitimate, or legal, cash income, whether it comes from your salary, profits, dividends, financial gifts, royalties, or unearned income. An offering is any amount above the tithe that you decide to give, or that the Spirit of God directs you to give. I am saying that if you are not a tither, you are not seeking first the Kingdom. Many times we ask God to bless us, but we don't qualify. If your first thought is to pay your bills and whatever is left you give to God, you aren't seeking first His Kingdom.

Your bills, house note, rent, grocery money, transportation, the education of your children, and all the other things you need money for should not be your first priority. God says to seek first the Kingdom, and make no mistake about it, He is talking about money. He says to give to His Kingdom first. Your first priority should be investing in God's work and God's Kingdom. Then, God's priority becomes *your* house note, *your* rent, *your* car payment, *your* grocery needs, *your* clothing needs, etc. That's why He says, *"You* seek first the Kingdom, and I will take care of the other things."

Many Christians, however, take care of themselves first and then "give God a tip." At the same time they cry out, "Bless me, Lord!" He can't bless them because they don't qualify for His blessing. Matthew 6:33 reads, *Seek first.* It doesn't read "seek second," and it doesn't read "think about Me after you do everything else with your money." Again, if you are not seeking Him *first,* you will not qualify for the blessing of the Lord.

WHAT ARE YOUR MOTIVES?

Here's God's second concern: **What are your motives?** Why do you want to prosper? Why do you want to be rich? Why do you want another job or a better job? Why do you want more money? Why do you want your own business? Why do you give offerings? Why? The why is very important. You can be a tither and a giver and still have wrong motives. I don't want to hurt anyone's feelings, but if the Word isn't working, something is wrong. The Word works all the time. It works for any person who will let it work.

Look at James 4:2-3:

You lust and do not have. You murder and covet and cannot obtain. You fight and war. Yet you do not have because you do not ask. You ask and do not receive [some people are asking and aren't getting], *because you ask amiss, that you may consume it on your pleasures.*

⚜

Remember, it takes money to spread the Gospel.

⚜

The word "amiss" means to ask badly. It means in an evil manner, diseased, or sick. Something is wrong in your asking. You ask God to bless you, but why are you asking?

Do you want more money so you can get a bigger house? Do you want an increase so you can get a nicer car? Why do you want a promotion and an increase on your job? Is it so you can obtain more things? Is it because you want to live a better lifestyle? If there is anything diseased in your asking, you won't receive. You are asking for more, but the reason you want more is selfish. It's not about the Kingdom. In other words, if God increased you with more, would *He* increase? If God gave you more money, would you increase your giving or just increase your lifestyle?

God blesses some individuals, but their giving doesn't increase. Just the house and car notes increase. If you increase and give less, that means the increase had nothing to do with God. You have to evaluate and consider honestly why you want riches, and why you want to prosper.

Look at Psalm 35:27:

Let them shout for joy and be glad, who favor my righteous cause; and let them say continually, "Let the Lord be magnified, who has pleasure in the prosperity of His servant."

True servants favor God's righteous cause. God says, "I have great pleasure in prospering those who serve Me, and the reason is because those who serve Me favor My righteous cause." A servant is someone who has voluntarily relinquished control of his life and has given himself over to the will of another. To serve God is to relinquish control of your life. The servant's will is irrelevant and immaterial. If you serve God, you relinquish the control of your will and serve His will. It's not about you, but it's about what He wants from you. What is God's righteous cause? What is God concerned about? John 3:16 says, *For God so loved the world that He gave His only begotten Son, that whoever believes in Him should not perish but have everlasting life.* Luke 19:10 says, *For the Son of Man has come to seek and to save that which was lost.*

Are you concerned about people getting saved? Remember, it takes money to spread the Gospel. As your finances increase, your giving should increase. However, if your motives are selfish, you will acquire so much debt that your ability to give into the Kingdom will be severely hindered, and if you are not giving into the Kingdom, God can't get involved in your life. I don't know about you, but I want God involved in my life. I want Him to increase me.

WHAT IS YOUR ATTITUDE?

Here's God's third concern: *What is your attitude?* God is concerned about your attitude. What is your attitude toward giving? What is your attitude toward other people? Let's talk about God for a minute. Isaiah 1:19 says, *If you are willing and obedient, you shall eat the good of the land.* Notice, this verse doesn't say just to be obedient. It says you have to be willing also. It is possible to do exactly what God tells you to do and not want to do it. The Bible says if you don't want to do it, you won't eat the good of the land. Notice, all through the Scriptures God talks about willing labor or a willing offering. You can't take money, throw it on the ground, and expect God to pick it up, but that's what we try to do. We give God something, but we throw it on the ground. God doesn't just want your obedience; He wants your willing obedience.

Second Corinthians 9:7 says, *So let each one give as he purposes in his heart, not grudgingly or of necessity; for God loves a cheerful giver.* God's concern here is not that you are merely giving, but rather *how* you are giving. He's concerned about your attitude. Do you give grudgingly? Are you giving, but you hate to do it? Do people have to put continuous pressure on you to give?

It is sad that some ministers on television spend forty minutes pleading for donations because many Christians will not give willingly. Many Christians even get upset at the ministers for spending so much time asking for money. But when the offering plate is passed, they won't give. Christian singers and musicians often record in secular venues because Christians won't support them. Many believers go to their concerts, jump and shout, yet only put in a dollar when the offering plate is passed. Then they wonder why those artists have stopped recording Christian music. It's because their fellow believers won't support anything until they are pressured into it.

What's your attitude toward people? God watches how you treat people and relate to them.

Look at Matthew 23:23:

"Woe to you, scribes and Pharisees, hypocrites! For you pay tithe of mint and anise and cummin, and have neglected the weightier matters of the law: justice and mercy and faith. These you ought to have done, without leaving the others undone."

Jesus says they should tithe, but they have omitted other important things. Notice these three things — judgment, mercy, and faith. Judgment is fairness. Are you fair with people, or are you a manipulator? Do you cheat people? If you own a business, do you make a fair profit? You have a right to a profit, but is it a fair profit? If you are in sales, is the product really what you say it is? You may say it's the best thing going, but is it really? If it's not,

God can't bless you. You have to be fair with people. Jesus says that if you don't have mercy, or if there's no compassion in your life, you cannot be blessed.

Are you faithful and trustworthy? Do you keep your word? When you make commitments, do you carry through on them? God can't bless a liar. Do you pay your bills? Fathers, do you pay your child support? If you aren't paying your child support, God can't bless you. You can't steal from your children and still expect God to bless you. Do you pay back borrowed money? Are you faithful?

God can't bless you if your attitude toward people is wrong. You cannot respect God and disrespect people. He said it Himself: "How can you say you love Me whom you haven't seen and yet hate your brother and you see him every day?" (See 1 John 4:20.) God connects Himself to people. The way you treat people is the way you treat God. You can't curse people and have God bless you.

Where Is Your Trust?

Here is God's fourth concern: **Where is your trust?**

Look at 1 Timothy 6:17-18:

Command those who are rich in this present age not to be haughty, nor to trust in uncertain riches but in the living God, who gives us richly all things to enjoy. Let them do good, that they be rich in good works, ready to give, willing to share.

Your trust is proven through your giving. Show me a man who trusts God, and I will show you a giver. Show me a man who has great trust in God, and I'll show you a great giver. It takes trust to let your money go. Fear holds on to money, but trust lets it go.

Remember, the Bible says prosperity will destroy a fool. Godly priorities, motives, attitude, and trust will keep you from being a fool.

Look at Luke 15:11-13:

Then He said: "A certain man had two sons. And the younger of them said to his father, 'Father, give me the portion of goods that falls to me.' So he divided to them his livelihood. And not many days after, the younger son gathered all together, journeyed to a far country, and there wasted his possessions with prodigal living."

You will waste the resources that God has given you whenever your priorities are off, your motives are impure, your attitude is wrong, and your trust is misplaced.

4
CHAPTER

God's Will for Your Life

For you know the grace of our
Lord Jesus Christ, that though He was
rich, yet for your sakes He became poor,
that you through His poverty might become rich.
2 Corinthians 8:9

In chapter 1, I established the fact that it's possible to prosper without sacrificing your relationship with God, your family, your church, your integrity, or your health. I also gave biblical examples of individuals whom God made rich.

In chapter 2, I dealt with cautions to those who become rich.

In chapter 3, I discussed God's concerns — our priorities, our motives, our attitude, and where we place our trust.

Now it's time to discuss God's will for your life. God wants you to be rich, not just to have your needs met. So let's examine what the Bible means when it uses the word "rich."

God will
always go
beyond what
you need.

Let's begin by looking at a very familiar verse, Philippians 4:19:

And my God shall supply all your need according to His riches in glory by Christ Jesus.

There are several things you need to notice in this verse.

Number one, God's status: *And my God shall supply all your need according to His riches. . . .* This verse implies that God is rich; His status is that of a rich person. If being rich were inherently wrong, then it would be wrong for God to be rich; but since God is both rich and holy, can't we be also?

Let's talk about the words "according to His riches," which mean the measure of His supply. We lose out on the magnificence of this wonderful verse because of our failure to understand the words "according to His riches." It does not say, "according to your job, according to your education, or according to the economy." It says He will supply your need "according to *His* riches in glory."

Also, it does not say He shall supply all your need "according to your need," but that's the way many people read it — "My God shall supply all my need according to my need." Supplying your need according to your need means that if you need $500, He will supply $500. It doesn't say that. It says, "according to His riches."

Notice, also, it doesn't say, "My God shall supply all your need *out* of His riches." This is a very important point because the words "according to" mean in conformity with or in a corresponding manner.

What's the difference? Well, let's say there are two multimillionaires. One gives $10,000 and the other gives $1 million to a church building project. The first one gave *out* of his riches. The second one gave *according to* his riches, or in conformity with and corresponding to how much he possessed. Because he possessed much, he gave more. The first multimillionaire simply reached in and gave something.

God will always go beyond what you need. *The Amplified Bible* states this beautifully: *And my God will liberally supply (fill to the full) your every need according to His riches in glory in Christ Jesus* (Philippians 4:19). It is God's will for you to be rich, not just to have your needs met.

First Timothy 6:17 says:

Command those who are rich in this present age not to be haughty, nor to trust in uncertain riches but in the living God, who gives us richly all things to enjoy.

The word "richly" means lavishly, abundantly, and copiously. Now, the *Phillip's Translation* says, [God] *generously gives us everything for our enjoyment.* The *Wuest Translation* says, *The One who is constantly offering us all things in a rich manner to enjoy.* We've seen in three different translations that it is God's will for us to experience abundance.

Now let's look at 2 Corinthians 8:9:

For you know the grace of our Lord Jesus Christ, that though He was rich, yet for your sakes He became poor, that you through His poverty might become rich.

Scripture teaches that Jesus was made to be sin though He didn't commit any sin. On the cross He was made to be sin, so we could have right standing with God. (See 2 Corinthians 5:21.) Scripture also says that He was made to be sick: *Himself took our infirmities and bore our sicknesses* (Matthew 8:17). He wasn't sick, but on the cross He bore our sicknesses so we could have healing, health, and long life. Scripture also says that He became poor. You couldn't get any poorer than He was on the cross. In fact, even His clothes were taken away from Him. He became poor so you could be rich. It doesn't say you *will* be rich. It says you *can* be rich.

Now how does the Bible define the word "rich"? The biblical definition of the word "rich" is summarized in 2 Corinthians 9:8, which reads:

And God is able to make all grace abound toward you, that you, always having all sufficiency in all things, may have an abundance for every good work.

The word "abound" means abundance, so we can summarize the word "rich" by using the word "abundance." Biblically speaking, being rich is to have an abundance of material resources for yourself personally and an abundance to give to the Kingdom of God and to the poor.

Now look at John 10:10:

The thief does not come except to steal, and to kill, and to destroy. I have come that they may have life, and that they may have it more abundantly.

The devil wants to steal and wreak havoc in your life. Jesus says that He has come that you may have life and have it more abundantly. "Abundance" means more than necessary, extraordinary, surpassing, to go beyond measure, to exceed what is needed, superabundant in quantity, and superior in quality. It also means wealth,

God wants your blessings to overflow — to run over.

affluence, overflow, and too much. We've seen God wants you to be rich and have more than just your needs met, and we've seen that "rich" means abundance, and "abundance" is having too much. Therefore, God wants you to have too much. Now if you can believe that, the following scriptures will make sense to you.

Look at Psalm 68:19:

Blessed be the Lord, who daily loads us with benefits, the God of our salvation! Selah.

If I were to point to a man and say, "He's loaded," most people would understand that the word "loaded" is a slang expression that means he has a lot of money. God wants you to be loaded. "Loaded" means to fill up, to supply in abundance, to supply in excess.

Now consider Malachi 3:10:

"Bring all the tithes into the storehouse, that there may be food in My house, and try Me now in this," says the Lord of hosts, "If I will not open for you the windows of heaven and pour out for you such blessing that there will not be room enough to receive it."

Many Christians can quote Malachi 3:10 by heart, but I want to emphasize the theme of excess — *there will not be room enough to receive it.* If we find a theme in Scripture that continues throughout the Bible, we know that's the will of God for us.

Look also at Luke 6:38:

"Give, and it will be given to you: good measure, pressed down, shaken together, and running over will be put into your bosom. For with the same measure that you use, it will be measured back to you."

God wants your blessings to overflow — to run over. Let me illustrate this truth: Take a pitcher of water and pour so much of it into a glass that the water runs over. Why does it run over? It is too much. Nothing runs over unless there's too much. God wants His blessings to overflow in your life.

Let's look at one final passage in 2 Corinthians 4:13:

And since we have the same spirit of faith, accord-
ing to what is written, "I believed and therefore I
spoke," we also believe and therefore speak.

That's the spirit of faith. The spirit of faith begins with
what is written in the Word. Once you find out what the
Bible says, believe it with your heart. Believing with the
heart means to trust God independent of your circumstances. Don't look at your bank account, don't look at
your bills, don't look at how much money you have
invested, and don't look at your pocketbook. In fact,
don't look at anything except God and His truth. To
believe with your heart is to base your beliefs on God's
Word, and then dare to say, or confess, what you believe
even before you see it. It is believing with your heart,
saying with your mouth, and acting on what you believe
that causes you to see the manifestation of faith.

Say this: **I believe I'm rich. I have abundance —
abundance in my personal life, abundance to give
to the Kingdom of God, abundance to give to the
needy, and abundance to give to the poor. I have
too much. I'm loaded! It's running over. There's
not enough room. I'm rich!**

5
CHAPTER

God's Priority

*Now may He who supplies seed to the sower,
and bread for food, supply and multiply
the seed you have sown and increase
the fruits of your righteousness.*
2 Corinthians 9:10

In this chapter we will deal with God's purpose. God is a God of purpose, so why does He want you and me to be rich? I believe we find part of the answer in John 10:10:

The thief does not come except to steal, and to kill, and to destroy. I have come that they may have life, and that they may have it more abundantly.

In the last chapter I gave you several definitions of the word "abundance," and I summarized them in two words — *too much.* Now I want to go back to two of those definitions because they will help open the door of understanding to God's purpose. The first definition is superior in quality. The second definition is super-abundant in quantity.

God loves others and He wants to bless them through you.

I believe there is a two-fold purpose involved in why God wants you to be rich. Let's deal with the first definition, superior in quality, while we look at the parable of the prodigal son. To paraphrase, the Bible says that a certain man had two sons. One son desired his inheritance prematurely, and his father gave it to him. This young man took the inheritance and squandered, or wasted it with riotous living.

In Luke 15:17-23 the Bible says that when he came to himself, he decided to go back to his father and repent. Right in the middle of the son's confession, the father said to his servants: *"Bring out the best robe and put it on him, and put a ring on his hand and sandals on his feet. And bring the fatted calf here and kill it, and let us eat and be merry; for this my son was dead and is alive again; he was lost and is found.' And they began to be merry"* (vv. 22-24).

REASON #1 FOR RICHES

Notice, the father said to bring forth the "best" because it was for his son. Here is the first reason why I think God wants you to be rich: **He is a good Father, and He wants the best for His children.** I believe it is the will of God for His children to have the best this life has to offer — the best in housing, transportation, clothing, food, education, vacation, and recreation. I believe it is the will of God for His children to live a first-class lifestyle, and I believe God is trying to find people who will believe that. It is going to take more than a minimum wage mentality for you to walk in God's best.

God is a God of purpose, and although He is concerned about you, He's also concerned about more than just you. In Luke 5:4-7 we have the story of the miraculous catch of fish. The Bible says that when Jesus finished teaching He spoke to Peter:

When He had stopped speaking, He said to Simon [Peter], "Launch out into the deep and let down your nets for a catch." But Simon answered and said to Him, "Master, we have toiled all night and caught nothing; nevertheless at Your word I will let down the net." And when they had done this, they caught a great number of fish, and their net was breaking. So they signaled to their partners in the other boat to come and help them. And they came and filled both the boats, so that they began to sink.

REASON #2 FOR RICHES

The word "abundance" also means superabundant in quantity, which leads us to the second purpose. The second reason why God wants you to be rich is **because God loves others and He wants to bless them through you.** The Scripture says that these fishermen filled both boats. Peter's partners were blessed because Peter had too much. God wants the Gospel of Jesus Christ to be taken to the world, so He is concerned about His work in the earth. God loves the lost, the sinners, the poor, the have-nots, the sick, the oppressed, and the elderly. He is concerned about the Kingdom of God in the earth being financed, and He needs to use you to finance it.

Now, I want to show you what I believe is a divine pattern from the Bible. In John 13 the Bible reveals that Jesus had a disciple named Judas who betrayed Him. At the last meal that the disciples ate before He was crucified, Jesus spoke briefly with Judas. The Bible says that Judas then got up from the table and went out.

Notice what it says in John 13:28-29:

But no one at the table knew for what reason He said this to him. For some thought, because Judas had the money box, that Jesus had said to him, "Buy those things we need for the feast," or that he should give something to the poor.

Judas was the staff treasurer, and the "money box" referred to the treasury. The disciples thought that Jesus said to him, *Buy those things we need for the feast,* or *give something to the poor.* This was the two-fold purpose for the money box: Either to buy items that the disciples needed, or to give money to the poor. I believe the purpose of the money box corresponds to the two-fold purpose God has in mind for prospering you. The first thing it says is to buy those things they needed, and that has to do with their personal well-being. To give something to the poor has to do with others. Which purpose is mentioned first? Notice that the personal well-being of the disciples is mentioned first.

Now let's go to 2 Corinthians 9:8. I am showing you from the Scripture what I believe to be a divine pattern. Here we see two of God's primary concerns.

And God is able to make all grace abound toward you, that you, always having all sufficiency in all things, may have an abundance for every good work.

This verse tells us that God is able to make all grace abound *toward you,* and it is His plan that you have an abundance for *every good work.* It is evident that God wants you to experience abundance in your personal life. It is also evident that God wants you to have an abundance to give into the Kingdom and to bless others. Again, which purpose is mentioned first? Your personal abundance ("all grace abound toward you").

Continuing on, let's look at 2 Corinthians 9:10:

Now may He who supplies [provides in abundance] *seed to the sower, and bread for food, supply and multiply the seed you have sown and increase the fruits of your righteousness.*

Again, there are two concerns. God says He will provide in abundance, *bread for your food* — which involves your personal well-being, and He also promises to *multiply the seed you have sown* — which involves your ability to give to the Kingdom. Again, which concern is mentioned first? Bread for your food. Can you see that there is no sacrifice in the perfect will of God?

He does not want you to experience lack in order to give into the Kingdom and bless others.

Next, let's look at 1 Timothy 6:17:

Command those who are rich in this present age not to be haughty, nor to trust in uncertain riches but in the living God, who gives us richly all things to enjoy.

To whom is God speaking in the latter part of this verse when He says, *who gives us richly all things to enjoy?* Clearly, it is all Christians, including you.

Look at verse 18:

Let them do good, that they be rich in good works, ready to give, willing to share.

Again, we see God's two concerns. We see God's concern for you — [He] *gives us richly all things to enjoy.* But then we see God is concerned about others and His work in the earth, as well — *Let them do good, that they be rich in good works, ready to give, willing to share.* One more time: Which concern is mentioned first? Notice, your well-being is mentioned first, as we have seen in four different scriptures.

Let's look at one more scripture in Mark 7. A Greek woman, a Gentile who wasn't a believer and didn't have a covenant with God, went to Jesus on behalf of her demon-possessed daughter. She went to Him because she knew He could help. This is what Jesus said to her in Mark 7:27:

But Jesus said unto her, "Let the children be filled first, for it is not good to take the children's bread and throw it to the little dogs."

Notice that Jesus says the children should be fed first. This story is also recorded in Matthew 15:24, and in this verse Jesus provides us with more insight into the matter of feeding the children of God first:

> Your personal abundance is vital to the extension of God's work in the earth.

"I was not sent except to the lost sheep of the house of Israel."

Now that seems strange to me. This woman is a Gentile, and Jesus said, *I was not sent except to the lost sheep of the house of Israel.* When He sends His disciples out in Matthew 10:5-6, He says, *"Do not go into the way of the Gentiles, and do not enter a city of the Samaritans. But go rather to the lost sheep of the house of Israel."*

However, John 3:16 says, *For God so loved the world. . . .* We know that God loves everyone. So why does Jesus say He isn't sent to them? Because God is a God of order. He always takes care of *His* house before He takes care of someone else's house. He says, *Let the children be filled first.*

Let's look at it this way: I am a proud parent of a son and a daughter. I love them both, and I love your children, as well. But when it comes to feeding, clothing, and educating children, I am going to take care of mine first. If your children get anything, it will be after I have taken care of my children. My house has to be fed first.

Read the following four points in light of what has already been shared.

Point 1: ***God's first priority is not others.*** It is not the lost (the sinners of the world). This may shock you, but God's first priority is not His work in the earth. *God's first priority is His own children.* When Jesus says that He isn't sent to the Gentiles, and He tells His disciples that they are not sent to the Gentiles, it isn't because He does not intend to reach the Gentiles. However, He wants to bless His people first, and they will be His vehicle, His channel, to bless the world. So, God's first priority is His very own children.

Point 2: ***Your first priority should not be yourself, but God's work in the earth.*** Matthew 6:33 says:

But seek first the kingdom of God and His righteousness, and all these things shall be added to you.

Again, your first priority should not be you. That's God's priority.

Point 3: ***Your personal abundance is vital to the extension of God's work in the earth.*** It takes money to spread the Gospel. If you don't know that, you haven't been around long. It takes money, but if you don't have it, you can't give it. How are you going to give something you don't have? And if you don't give it, God's work is hindered. If God's family cannot support His work in the earth, who is going to do it? We are supposed to finance God's work, but we can't do it if we don't have a surplus.

Point 4: ***When you obey God's laws that govern riches in the Kingdom, two things happen — your personal needs and desires that are consistent with a godly life will be met, and God's work in the earth will be financed.*** Everyone will be happy and everyone will be blessed.

The central issue is: *Do you want to go God's way? Then seek first the Kingdom of God and His way of doing things.*

6
CHAPTER

The Law of Renewal

Beloved, I pray that you may prosper in all things
and be in health, just as your soul prospers.
3 John 2

There are six laws that govern riches in the Kingdom of God:

1) The Law of Renewal

2) The Law of Giving and Receiving

3) The Law of Words

4) The Law of Obedience

5) The Law of Love

6) The Law of Growth and Progression

The Law of Renewal deals with your thinking, the Law of Giving and Receiving with your money, the Law of Words with your mouth, the Law of Obedience with the Holy Spirit, the Law of Love with relationships, and the Law of Growth and Progression with patience.

In establishing the Law of Renewal, let's look at Romans 12:2:

Before you can prosper in God, you will have to change in regard to handling your finances.

And do not be conformed to this world, but be transformed by the renewing of your mind, that you may prove what is that good and acceptable and perfect will of God.

There are three questions we need to answer about the Law of Renewal:

1) What is mind renewal?
2) Why is mind renewal so important?
3) How is the mind renewed?

WHAT IS MIND RENEWAL?

The word "renew" means to make new. It means to renovate. When you renovate anything, you have to go in and tear out the old and replace it with something new. It also means an exchange that leads to change, exchanging your way of thinking for God's way of thinking, which will lead to a change in behavior. Once your behavior is changed, your life will change.

Another scripture that addresses mind renewal is Isaiah 55:7:

Let the wicked forsake his way, and the unrighteous man his thoughts; let him return to the Lord, and He will have mercy on him; and to our God, for He will abundantly pardon.

Before you can prosper in God, you will have to change in regard to handling your finances. For one thing, you will have to change any impulsive buying tendencies you may have, especially if you are the type of person who walks into a store and objects start talking to you, "Buy me . . . buy me." You must budget your finances and have a spending plan. Stop living off of credit. You're going to have to deal with some impatience as these changes are instituted in your life and get rid of the "I've-got-to-have-it-now" mentality. You must stop trying to keep up with the Joneses. You may not know this, but the Joneses filed for bankruptcy last year!

You must help your children overcome peer pressure, as well. There are Christian families who are struggling financially and yet they try to buy a $160 pair of sneakers for their child. This is simply ludicrous! Spouses should stop making unilateral decisions and stop operating like they are single. (*My* bills, *your* bills, *my* note, *your* note, *my* money, *your* money.) Apart from an unresolved trust issue that necessitates the division of resources, this practice mitigates a couple's power to achieve financial goals.

You have to change any workaholic mentality that may exist and change any stinginess mentality, as well. You have to change the spend-every-penny mentality and learn how to save money.

In Isaiah 55:8, notice how God connects *ways* to *thoughts:*

"For My thoughts are not your thoughts, nor are your ways My ways. . . ."

God places thoughts ahead of ways. Do you know why thoughts are mentioned first? Because you eventually live out your thought patterns. What you think comes out in your behavior. A person's behavior does not change until his thinking changes.

In Isaiah 55:9-11 God continues by saying:

"For as the heavens are higher than the earth, so are My ways higher than your ways, and My thoughts than your thoughts. For as the rain comes down, and the snow from heaven, and do not return there, but water the earth, and make it bring forth and bud, that it may give seed to the sower and bread to the eater, so shall My word be. . . ."

God's Word reveals His thoughts. If you want to know what God thinks on a matter, go to His Word. The Bible is a book that contains God's thoughts.

"So shall My word be that goes forth from My mouth; it shall not return to Me void, but it shall accomplish what I please, and it shall prosper in the thing for which I sent it . . . Instead of the thorn shall come up the cypress tree, and instead of the brier shall come up the myrtle tree. . . ."

Isaiah 55:11,13

Again, mind renewal is an exchange that leads to change. Exchanging your thoughts for God's thoughts will lead to a change in your behavior, and a change in your behavior will result in a changed lifestyle. You will move from an unproductive life to one that is fruitful and productive.

Why Is Mind Renewal So Important?

Third John 2 reads:

Beloved, I pray that you may prosper in all things and be in health, just as your soul prospers.

John says that mind renewal leads to the prosperity of the soul. The soul is your mind, your emotions, and your will. Think about this: If the soul can be prosperous, then it can also be poor. We call a poor soul a poverty mind-set. Scripture says, *Prosper in all things and be in health, just as your soul prospers.* The words "just as" mean to the degree, or directly proportionate. Look at it this way: To the degree that your soul prospers, you will prosper in life.

Proverbs 23:7 reads:

For as he thinks in his heart, so is he. . . .

Numbers 13:33 reads:

"There we saw the giants (the descendants of Anak came from the giants); and we were like grasshoppers in our own sight, and so we were in their sight."

I want to give you three principles that I've discovered in these two scriptures.

Principle 1: ***Inward change produces lasting outward change.*** If you want to change a man's life, you don't start with his environment, and you don't start with the external part of the man. You start on the inside of a man. You can take a man — black, white, red, yellow, or brown — out of a poor environment and put him into a wealthy environment, and if that man is poor on the inside, then he will find a way to change his environment to accommodate his thinking.

It is unfortunate that some of our professional athletes make so much money, and down the road you find many of them struggle financially. And did you know that most people who win the lottery don't maintain their wealth? Do you know why they don't? Because lasting outward change is a product of inward change, not a product of financial gain.

Principle 2: *A person's consistent, outward condition is a reflection of his consistent, inward condition.* So, if you are consistently struggling financially, this reflects a consistent state of mental poverty.

Principle 3: *You act in harmony with what you believe or think about yourself.*

Those ten men in Numbers 13:33 who said, *We were like grasshoppers,* didn't fight a single giant. It wasn't the giants that kept them out of the Promised Land, but their own inward disposition and thoughts. Remember, as a man thinks in his heart, so is he.

HOW IS THE MIND RENEWED?

Mind renewal is a process, not an event; it does not happen instantaneously. It requires great effort. What is your commitment to mind renewal? I am not asking about your love for God, your commitment to giving, or your church attendance. I am asking about your personal commitment to mind renewal. Let's look at 2 Corinthians 10:4-5 to clarify something I believe will be a blessing to you.

For the weapons of our warfare are not carnal but mighty in God for pulling down of strongholds, casting down arguments [the *King James Version* says *"imaginations"*] *and every high thing that exalts itself against the knowledge of God, bringing every thought into captivity to the obedience of Christ.*

Let's look at the word "imagination." "Imagination" means human reasoning. Remember what the Lord said in Isaiah 55:8: "Your thoughts are not My thoughts." Any thought you have that is inconsistent with the way God thinks is a result of human reasoning. The Bible says that you have to cast down human reasoning or anything that exalts itself against the knowledge of God. That word "imagination" comes from the root word "image." What is an image? It's a mental picture. God created us to think in pictures. If I say, "big, mean dog," you don't see in your mind the words "big," "mean," and "dog." No, the moment I say, "big, mean dog" you have an image of a dog that is big and mean, like a Doberman pinscher, because we don't think in words; we think in pictures or images.

Here is the challenge: You can never live beyond the mental image you have on the inside of you. There is a mental picture on the inside that you have about your life, yourself, and your finances. You cannot live beyond that. Some Christians cannot see themselves putting $1,000 in the offering plate or living in certain upscale communities. Some cannot see themselves as supervisors on their jobs or owning a prosperous business. Remember, you cannot have what you cannot see. If you have a negative self-image, it must be changed.

In 2 Corinthians 10:4, when God talks about strongholds, He is not referring to demons, but thoughts or "mind castles." A stronghold is a certain way of thinking that has been established over a period of time, fortified by custom, tradition, or habit, and resistant to change. A stronghold is established brick by brick, thought by thought, and then it develops into a mind-set. Even though we were changed in our spirits instantaneously, our minds were unaffected by the new birth. So, we come into the Kingdom of God with an inferior way of thinking, a worldly way of thinking, a carnal way of thinking, a way that is inconsistent with the Scriptures.

This mental conditioning happens through several different factors, but the home environment is mainly to blame. What type of environment were you raised in? What kind of community was it? What type of school did you attend, especially when you were young? What about the authority figures in your life — coaches, teachers, and especially your parents? What did your parents think about money and prosperity? Your answers to these questions are very important because it is normal to automatically embrace your parents' ways of thinking. What have you heard over and over again? What kinds of things have you internalized about money, wealth, and possessions? What kinds of experiences have you had?

All of these things have contributed to a mind-set the Bible calls a stronghold. You don't develop beliefs and deeply rooted thoughts overnight. This happens over a period of years. Even when you got saved, you still had an unsaved mind. That is why it is necessary for you to saturate yourself with biblical teaching in this area to try to correct what has happened over the years, especially concerning financial matters. One message won't get the job done, and one series of messages won't erase years of erroneous thinking.

Forget about what you think. Find out what God thinks.

Again, how is the mind renewed? Look at James 1:21:

Therefore lay aside all filthiness and overflow of wickedness, and receive with meekness the implanted word, which is able to save your souls.

That's the answer to mind renewal. James calls mind renewal the salvation of the soul, which implies your soul didn't get saved when you got saved. So how do you get your mind renewed? *Receive with meekness the implanted word* — which means to be teachable, to have a humble spirit, and to lose your old mind.

Look at Philippians 2:5:

Let this mind be in you which was also in Christ Jesus.

Forget about what you think. Find out what God thinks. Notice, mind renewal is connected to God's Word. Apart from the Word there can be no mind renewal, and apart from the Word there can be no salvation of the soul. Mind renewal is not connected to giving money. Giving will be the by-product of a renewed mind, but it is possible to give and not have your mind renewed. That's what has happened to many Christians. They were giving, but their giving had no life in it. The life is in the seed. The giving is like the husk around the seed, but the Word is the seed.

I know some Christians who give and wonder why they have not received a harvest. Giving doesn't renew your mind. It is the Word that renews your mind, and not just the Word, but the *implanted Word.* The metaphor is that of a seed taking root in the ground. We have the Word, but it has no roots, and we aren't rooted in it. We were rooted in a lot of other stuff over the years, but now we've got to get rooted in the Word. We can't just hear the Word; we have to get the Word planted in our hearts.

Consider Luke 8:11:

The seed is the word of God.

Mark 4:26 says:

The kingdom of God is as if a man should scatter seed on the ground.

The seed is the Word of God, but we must scatter the seed on the ground. The ground is the human spirit or the heart of man.

Do you qualify for a financial harvest?

Let me give you three truths.

Truth 1: *No planting, no harvest.* The seed is the Word of God. Even if you give money, you must also plant the Word of God in your heart. You plant the Word of God by hearing His Word and speaking it out of your mouth. If you don't plant the Word of God in your heart, you will not receive a harvest from God's Word.

Truth 2: *If you sow sparingly you will reap sparingly, but if you sow bountifully you will reap bountifully.* If you spend much time hearing and speaking God's Word, then you will receive much from God's Word; however, if you only spend a little time hearing and speaking God's Word, you will only receive a small crop.

Truth 3: *Different kinds of seeds produce different kinds of crops.* If you want a tomato harvest, you have to plant tomato seeds. If you want a flower garden, you have to plant flower seeds.

You wouldn't even think about planting collard green seeds to get flowers or tomato seeds to get collard greens. If you want healing for your body, you must listen to tapes and read books that clearly declare that healing is God's will for everyone. There are Christians who are believing for healing, but they are not planting the Word of God regarding healing. If you want a prosperous marriage, you have to listen to tapes, attend marriage retreats, and read books on the subject of marriage. If you want financial prosperity, you must listen to tapes, attend lecture and teaching seminars, and read books that declare financial prosperity is the will of God for every believer. You must sow purposefully because different kinds of seeds produce different kinds of crops.

Here is an important question: Do you qualify for a financial harvest, or do you have a misguided and unreasonable expectation? If you go to the bank for a loan, you've got to meet certain qualifications. In the last three months, how many books have you read on finances and material prosperity? How many tapes have you listened to, and how many videos or DVDs have you watched in this area? It's no different than expecting tomatoes to grow in your backyard without ever planting a tomato seed.

7

CHAPTER

The Law of Giving and Receiving

There is one who scatters, yet increases more;
and there is one who withholds more
than is right, but it leads to poverty.
The generous soul will be made rich, and
he who waters will also be watered himself.
Proverbs 11:24-25

We have already learned that there are six laws that govern riches in the Kingdom of God: The Law of Renewal, the Law of Giving and Receiving, the Law of Words, the Law of Obedience, the Law of Love, and the Law of Growth and Progression.

In this chapter we discuss the Law of Giving and Receiving. First, let's examine Philippians 4:15:

Now you Philippians know also that in the begin-
ning of the gospel, when I departed from
Macedonia, no church shared with me concerning
giving and receiving but you only.

And 1 Kings 17:8-16:

Then the word of the Lord came unto him [Elijah], *saying, "Arise, go to Zarephath, which belongs to Sidon, and dwell there. See, I have commanded a widow there to provide for you." So he arose and went to Zarephath. And when he came to the gate of the city, indeed a widow was there gathering sticks. And he called to her and said, "Please bring me a little water in a cup, that I may drink." And as she was going to get it, he called to her and said, "Please bring me a morsel of bread in your hand." So she said, "As the Lord your God lives, I do not have bread, only a handful of flour in a bin, and a little oil in a jar; and see, I am gathering a couple of sticks that I may go in and prepare it for myself and my son, that we may eat it, and die." And Elijah said to her, "Do not fear; go and do as you have said, but make me a small cake from it first, and bring it to me; and afterward make some for yourself and your son. For thus says the Lord God of Israel: 'The bin of flour shall not be used up, nor shall the jar of oil run dry, until the day the Lord sends rain on the earth.'" So she went away and did according to the word of Elijah; and she and he and her household ate for many days. The bin of flour was not used up, nor did the jar of oil run dry, according to the word of the Lord which He spoke by Elijah.*

THREE CHARACTERISTICS OF THIS LAW

The Law of Giving and Receiving has three primary characteristics.

Characteristic 1: *Everything produces after its kind.* This law is found in Genesis 1:11-12, which states:

> *Then God said, "Let the earth bring forth grass, the herb that yields seed, and the fruit tree that yields fruit according to its kind, whose seed is in itself, on the earth"; and it was so. And the earth brought forth grass, the herb that yields seed according to its kind, and the tree that yields fruit, whose seed is in itself according to its kind. And God saw that it was good.*

> It is not wrong to expect to receive.

If you plant apple seeds, they will produce apples. Human seeds produce humans. Love seeds produce love. Hate seeds produce hate. Money seeds produce money. In the story we cited from 1 Kings, the woman gave food to the prophet and, as a result, she received a harvest of food.

Characteristic 2: *God uses what you have to bless others, and then He multiplies your giving back to you.* The woman in 1 Kings gave food to the servant of God, who represented the work of God in the earth. God used the food that she gave to bless His work, then multiplied the food that was given back to her. We see the principle of multiplication even in nature. If you sow a kernel of corn seed, you don't receive one kernel in return. There is a multiplication process. You sow a kernel but reap a stalk with many ears on it, and each ear has many kernels on it.

Characteristic 3: *In the mind of God, giving and receiving are inseparable.* The Law of Giving and Receiving is like a coin. It has a head side and a tail side. It is impossible for me to give you the head side without giving you the tail side of the coin. That is the way the Law of Giving and Receiving operates.

OBSERVATIONS ABOUT THESE CHARACTERISTICS

Now, I want to make some observations regarding these three characteristics. Remember, the three characteristics are: 1) everything produces after its kind, 2) God uses what you give to bless others and then He multiplies the return on what you gave back to you, and 3) in the mind of God, giving and receiving are inseparable.

It is not wrong to expect to receive. Oftentimes we hear Christians say, "Well, I give but I don't expect to receive." That's not humility, it's not biblical, and it contradicts the Law of Giving and Receiving. It's scriptural to give in anticipation of receiving. Elijah told the widow woman to bake him a cake first, with the promise that she would receive a supernatural supply. Remember that God is speaking through the prophet

Elijah. God is not obligated to make a promise to her. He could have said, "Give because I told you to do so." He did not have to connect a promise "to receive" to His command, but He wanted her to receive. So there is nothing wrong with having an expectation to receive. In fact, it is wrong not to expect to receive when you give.

When receiving is connected to giving, fear is overcome. When Elijah instructed the woman to give, he did not just say, *"give."* In effect, he said, "Give to me *first,* and receive." (*"The bin of flour shall not be used up, nor shall the jar of oil run dry, until the day the Lord sends rain on the earth,"* 1 Kings 17:14.) Here we see a clear illustration of the Law of Giving and Receiving. When God instructs you to give, He couples that command with a promise or an entitlement to receive. It is the entitlement to receive that destroys the fear of giving.

The Law of Giving and Receiving is unaffected by the economy. Right in the midst of a three-and-a-half-year famine, the widow woman's needs were met.

Now, we are in a critical time in our country. God told me that economic upheaval was coming. He didn't say there would be a recession. He said there would be economic upheaval, but the good news is that His laws are unaffected by the financial fluctuations in the economy. Those who stand on God's Word don't have to worry about a thing. Some Christians have their trust in the wrong place. They have placed their trust in jobs, or in their money in the bank, but hundreds of thousands of people are being laid off, companies are closing, and investors are losing their money.

> The Law of Giving and Receiving is an unchanging lifestyle principle.

"Are you saying that if I stand on the Word, I won't get laid off?"

No, I am not saying that, but I am saying that for those who stand on the Word, if you get laid off, God will open another door of opportunity. Those who think this is just a game or a gimmick are going to be at a financial disadvantage.

Look at what Jesus said in Luke 6:46-48:

"But why do you call Me 'Lord, Lord,' and not do the things which I say? Whoever comes to Me, and hears My sayings and does them. I will show you whom he is like: He is like a man building a house, who dug deep and laid the foundation on the rock. And when the flood arose, the stream beat vehemently against that house, and could not shake it; for it was founded on the rock."

If you are operating in the Law of Giving and Receiving, your financial position is secure.

FOUR WAYS TO ACTIVATE THIS LAW

There are four major ways we can activate the Law of Giving and Receiving.

Through tithes and offerings. (Malachi 3:8.) The tithe is 10 percent of all legitimate income. Offerings are anything above that 10 percent.

Through giving to the poor. Proverbs 19:17 tells us those who give to the poor lend to the Lord, and the Lord will pay them back. Proverbs 28:27 tells us when a person gives to the poor, he or she will not lack. In Matthew 6:4, to those who give alms, the Bible promises an open reward. Notice each command is coupled with a promise to receive.

By giving under the direction of Jesus or the Holy Spirit. Luke 6:38 says, *"Give, and it will be given to you: good measure, pressed down, shaken together, and running over will be put into your bosom. . . ."*

By giving to those who minister God's Word to you. (For example, the Sunday school teacher, the small group leader, the pastor, etc.) In Galatians 6:6-9, God promises you will receive a financial return.

A LIFESTYLE PRINCIPLE

The Law of Giving and Receiving is an unchanging lifestyle principle. Notice these words from Genesis 8:22: *"While the earth remains, seedtime and harvest, cold and heat, winter and summer, and day and night shall not cease."* Often, when we read 1 Kings 17:8-16, we think the woman brought the prophet a little cake only one time. No, that famine lasted three-and-a-half years. She brought him a cake first every day over the duration of the three-and-a-half years. It is a lifestyle principle, not an event.

A PARADOX

The Law of Giving and Receiving is a paradox. A paradox is that which is seemingly contradictory, or opposed to common sense, but nevertheless true. This law appears to be contradictory and appears to make no sense.

> *Start where you are. Don't measure your level of giving by anyone else's standards.*

Let me show you what I mean. In Proverbs 11:24-25 it says:

> *There is one who scatters, yet increases more; and there is one who withholds more than is right, but it leads to poverty. The generous soul will be made rich, and he who waters will also be watered himself.*

That is a paradox — the man who scatters will increase, and the one who withholds will end up in poverty.

The Living Bible says, *It is possible to give away and become richer!* That doesn't make sense to the natural mind. *It is also possible to hold on too tightly and lose everything. Yes, the liberal man shall be rich! By watering others, he waters himself.* What kind of sense does that make?

In order to get watered, I have to water you. In order to have, I have to give. This concept of releasing in order to gain challenges the logical mind. Satan will try to put pressure on you to hold on to your money because he knows that when you hold on to it, you are going to lose it. This is a paradox. In order to get richer you have to give; in order to have you have to give. So, if you don't want to have anything, hold on to your money. Here, this woman has a little oil in a jar, just enough to make a little cake. The Bible says that she and her son were going to eat it and die. Guess what the prophet said? If you want to survive, start giving it away. That's a paradox, and it is opposed to what we call common sense, but as a result of her obedience, she survived the famine.

START WHERE YOU ARE

Start where you are. God's measuring unit is a percentage, not an exact amount. I'm talking about giving, not the tithe. The tithe is always 10 percent. Start where you are. Don't measure your level of giving by anyone else's standards. God is not asking you to do what everyone else is doing. What did Elijah tell that woman? He said, *Make me a small cake from it first.* He didn't ask her for a lot because she didn't have a lot. You can't wait until you get much. It doesn't work like that. You have to give the little that you have.

It's not the Law of Receiving and Giving; it's the Law of Giving and Receiving. In Mark 12:41-43, as Jesus sat at the treasury watching the rich people putting their money in the collection box, He observed a widow who put in two mites. (*The Revised Standard Version* of the

Bible says they were two copper coins worth the equivalent of one penny.) Jesus looked at the woman and called His disciples over and said, "See that woman right there, that little woman who gave those two mites. She has given more than all the rest." What kind of sense does that make? We know it wasn't the quantity she gave that meant so much to Him. Rather, it was the quality of her giving. God measured what she gave against what she had to give, but she had to start where she was.

GOD WILL PROVIDE SEED TO SOW

God provides resources to Christians who mix faith with His Word. (Hebrews 4:2.) If you are a Word-believing Christian, God will provide money for you to give.

Look at 2 Corinthians 9:10:

Now may He who supplies seed to the sower, and bread for food, supply and multiply the seed you have sown and increase the fruits of your righteousness.

This scripture says God will provide you with seed to sow. So, don't ever again say, "I don't have any money to give." When you say with your mouth, "I don't have any money to give," or "I can't afford to give," you are calling God a liar. I know you don't mean to call God a liar, but that is what you're doing. He said He would provide you with seed to sow, and if you are a Word-believing Christian, you must have faith in that verse. You don't have a money problem. You may think you do, but you don't. However, you may have a faith problem, which means you simply don't believe the Bible.

Let me show you how to obtain money to give.

First, ask for money to give. Say, "Father, I desire money to give based on 2 Corinthians 9:10."

Second, believe you receive the money to give based on Mark 11:24.

Third, bind Satan's power over your money, according to Matthew 16:19. Say, "Satan, I bind you in the name of Jesus. You will not hinder money from coming to me."

Fourth, loose the angels according to Hebrews 1:13-14. Say, "Go, ministering spirits, and bring me money to give."

Finally, thank God every day. Say, "Father, I thank You. I believe I have received money to give in the name of Jesus."

You will be amazed at what God will put into your hands.

8
CHAPTER

The Law of Words

"Brood of vipers! How can you, being evil,
speak good things? For out of the abundance
of the heart the mouth speaks."
Matthew 12:34

The Word of God teaches there is a connection between the words we speak and the success or failure we experience in our lives. This refers to every aspect of our lives — spiritual, mental, physical, social, and financial. However, this is a book about finances, so we're going to focus on the financial and material realms.

In this chapter I want to teach you how to control your speech so your words will work for you, not against you. The Bible says in the mouth of two or three witnesses every word is established, but I'm going to go beyond what is required and give you four witnesses.

Notice Proverbs 18:20-21:

A man's stomach shall be satisfied from the fruit of his mouth; from the produce of his lips he shall be filled. Death and life are in the power of the tongue, and those who love it will eat its fruit.

> There is a connection between the words we speak and the success or failure we experience in our lives.

This text teaches us that spoken words are like seeds — bad or good — that produce a harvest. It also teaches us that spoken words are containers of death and life, and we either speak death to our lives or life to our lives.

Again, verse 20 says, *A man's stomach shall be satisfied from the fruit of his mouth; from the produce of his lips he shall be filled.* The *Amplified Bible* says, *And with the consequence of his words he must be satisfied [whether good or evil].* The *New English Version* of the Bible says, *A man may live by the fruit of his tongue, his lips may earn him a livelihood.*

Let's examine Matthew 6:30-31:

"Now if God so clothes the grass of the field, which today is, and tomorrow is thrown into the oven, will He not much more clothe you, O you of little faith? Therefore do not worry, saying, 'What shall we eat?' or 'What shall we drink?' or 'What shall we wear?'"

There are two main things we need to notice from this text.

One: ***You don't have a money problem; you have a faith problem.*** Notice, when talking about material things, Jesus doesn't say, "O you of little money." He says, "O you of little faith." You may think you have a money problem, but you don't. You have a faith problem.

Two: *Faith and fear are released by the words of your mouth.* The words you speak on a daily basis release faith or fear. People worry because they are fearful. They're afraid of lack, afraid of not having enough, afraid of not being able to pay their bills, afraid of going in debt, afraid of bankruptcy. How did Jesus know that they were worried? He knew based on what they were saying. Jesus says, *Therefore do not worry, saying.* . . . In effect He is saying, "Don't meditate on negative thoughts of insufficiency, shortage, or lack, and don't speak them."

Thoughts of insufficiency, shortage, or lack may come to your mind, but don't receive them. Don't say what you don't have, or what you can't afford, or what you can't do. When you speak a negative thought, you give life to it. That's why Proverbs 30:32 says, *If you have devised evil, put your hand on your mouth.* You can easily see the relationship of that verse to Matthew 12:33:

"Either make the tree good and its fruit good, or else make the tree bad and its fruit bad; for a tree is known by its fruit."

The word "tree" refers to the words of your mouth. The word "fruit" refers to your consistent circumstances, or the quality of your life. So, it says to make the words of your mouth good, and then your consistent circumstances, or the quality of your life, will be good. Or make the words of your mouth bad (corrupt or negative), and then your consistent circumstances, or the quality of your life, will be bad. For the tree — that's the character and nature of the words you speak — is known by its fruit — the quality of your life.

I don't have to be with you every day to listen to the words of your mouth. I can look at your consistent circumstances, or I can look at the quality of your life, and they will tell me what kind of words you are speaking.

Matthew 12:34 says:

"Brood of vipers! How can you, being evil, speak good things? For out of the abundance of the heart the mouth speaks."

Whatever is in your heart in abundance will come out of your mouth. If television programs are in your heart in abundance, you're going to quote television characters. If the Word of God is in your heart in abundance, you're going to verbalize the Bible. Remember when you were hammering and hit your finger by accident, and those curse words came out of your mouth? Do you know why those words came out of your mouth? They were in your heart! Whenever you experience pressure in your life, you're going to say what's in your heart.

Jesus continues in Matthew 12:35:

"A good man out of the good treasure of his heart brings forth good things, and an evil man out of the evil treasure brings forth evil things."

You will reveal what is in your heart. If you deposit God's Word in your heart, you will bring forth good things. If you don't deposit God's Word in your heart, you're going to bring forth evil things. Words are go-getters. They "go and get" whatever you speak with your mouth.

Jesus continues in Matthew 12:36:

"But I say to you that for every idle word men may speak, they will give account of it in the day of judgment."

God will hold us accountable for every idle word we speak — that is, every unproductive, careless, thought-less, negative word. "I can't give" are idle words. "I can't afford" are idle words. These are words that don't work for us, and God calls them idle words. We're going to have to give an account of our words.

We conclude the text from Matthew 12 with verse 37:

"For by your words you wilt be justified, and by your words you will be condemned."

Sometime just take a moment to listen to the words that are coming out of your mouth. You may discover you talk so much that you don't even hear what you're saying. Remember, there's a connection between the words you speak and the quality of life you experience.

BELIEVING AND SPEAKING IN AGREEMENT WITH GOD'S WORD

Pay attention to these words from Mark 11:12-14, 20-24:

Now the next day, when they had come out from Bethany, He was hungry. And seeing from afar a fig tree having leaves, He went to see if perhaps He would find something on it. When He came to it, He found nothing but leaves, for it was not the season for figs. In response Jesus said to it, "Let no one eat fruit from you ever again." And His disciples heard it . . . Now in the morning, as they passed by, they saw the fig tree dried up from the roots. And Peter, remembering, said to Him, "Rabbi, look! The fig tree which You cursed has withered away." So Jesus answered and said to them, "Have faith in God. For assuredly I say to you, whoever says to this mountain, 'Be removed and be cast into the sea,' and does not doubt in his heart, but believes that those things he says will be done, he will have whatever he says. Therefore I say to you, whatever things you ask when you pray, believe that you receive them, and you will have them."

Jesus is making several vital points here.

Point 1: ***Don't curse your situation.*** Jesus had a need. He was hungry. He went to the tree to get figs, but no figs were on the tree. The Bible says He cursed the tree. That was an object lesson. He was saying whenever you have a need, and it appears the need is not being met, *don't* curse your situation. Don't start speaking negatively over your situation. For example, if you have a hardheaded child, don't start calling him "hardheaded."

Point 2: *Dare to speak your faith.* Jesus told us not to be afraid or intimidated by men. Jesus spoke to the tree audibly and the disciples heard it. Here Jesus is teaching us the importance of speaking your faith even though others may not understand what you are doing. Most people don't understand how faith works, but don't let that intimidate you.

Point 3: *Your present condition in life is the result of words you consistently spoke in the past.* When the disciples looked at the dried-up tree, it was obvious that the present condition of the tree was directly related to the words Jesus spoke the day before.

Point 4: *Your faith-filled words are producing results even when you see no change in the natural realm.* When Jesus spoke to that tree, from a natural standpoint it appeared nothing happened. But below the surface of the ground, that tree began to dry up. I'm saying even though you see no apparent change, your faith-filled words are working all the time.

Point 5: *You must believe God's Word with your heart and dare to speak to the mountain.* You have to speak to the challenge, to the shortage, to the insufficiency, to the debt, or to the unemployment.

Point 6: *You should only speak your desires.* Jesus said a man shall have *whatever he says.* Now if you're going to have whatever you say — good or bad — shouldn't you speak your desires?

Point 7: **You have to believe and speak like you already have it before you get it.**

Now take a good look at Romans 4:17:

(As it is written, "I have made you a father of many nations") in the presence of Him whom he believed — God, who gives life to the dead and calls those things which do not exist as though they did.

The Bible says you are to call things that are not manifested as though they were manifested, but that's not what most folks normally do. Instead, people tend to call things that are as though they are. Or, they may call things that are as though they are not. Most Christians either "tell it like it is," or they operate in denial.

Let's say in the natural you don't have enough money to pay your bills. What do you say in such a situation? You say, "I can't pay my bills." That's telling it like it is. Let's say you don't have transportation. What do you say? You say, "I don't have transportation." That's telling it like it is. What's wrong with telling it like it is? Remember, you want to change your circumstances. When you tell it like it is, you establish, maintain, and solidify your circumstances. It is insanity to do the same thing and expect different results. In other words, you cannot keep rehearsing the problem and expect it to miraculously improve.

On the other end of the spectrum, there are Christians who confuse faith with denial. Their bills are overdue, and they say, "I don't have any bills." The mortgage payment is due, but they say, "I don't have a mortgage payment due." The phone rings and a creditor is calling, but they say, "Creditor? What creditor?" That's denial. Faith does not deny the existence of problems.

God said to call those things that are not manifested as though they were. (See Romans 4:17.) Find out what God says and repeat what He says as though it has already happened. You have to say what the Bible says about your circumstances because Jesus says you have to believe you have it before you get it.

Look now at 2 Corinthians 4:13:

And since we have the same spirit of faith, according as what is written, "I believed and therefore I spoke," we also believe and therefore speak.

Let's say you have a pressing need, but you don't have the resources to meet that need. Philippians 4:19 says, *And my God shall supply all your need. . . .* That's what is written, but it's not what is manifested. You want what is written to be manifested, right? Based on the Scripture, you should say, "I believe all my needs are met according to His riches in glory by Christ Jesus." You're saying what you believe. That's how you got saved.

This is clearly declared in Romans 10:9-10:

That if you confess with your mouth the Lord Jesus and believe in your heart that God has raised Him from the dead, you will be saved. For with the heart one believes unto righteousness, and with the mouth confession is made unto salvation.

When you were saved, you called things that were not as though they were. When you prayed the sinner's prayer, you weren't saved. You were a sinner, and you called Jesus your Lord. It was calling those things that were not as though they were which caused you to be born again.

Some say that walking by faith is hard, but it's not hard. You do it all the time. You call things that are not as though they are all the time.

Here's an example: When you go out to the backyard to feed the dog, you call things that are not as though they were. You say, "Here, Boy. Here, Boy," but you don't see the dog. You don't say, "There, Boy." You don't say, "Boy's not here, Boy's not here." You say, "Here, Boy. Here, Boy." The dog may be down the street or in a neighbor's yard, but you are saying "Here, Boy" to bring the dog to you. Just as you would call the dog you cannot see, you should call the unmanifested desire to you. If you keep talking about your problem, you'll never change it. Stop verbalizing your lack and your fear.

CONTROLLING YOUR WORDS

Let's look at James 3:1-5:

My brethren, let not many of you become teachers, knowing that we shall receive a stricter judgment. For we all stumble in many things. If anyone does not stumble in word [in speech], *he is a perfect man, able also to bridle the whole body. Indeed, we put bits in the horses' mouths that they may obey us, and we turn their whole body. Look also at ships: although they are so large and are driven by fierce winds, they are turned by a very small rudder wherever the pilot desires. Even so the tongue. . . .*

James uses the illustration of turning a powerful horse with a small bit in its mouth, and turning an entire ship in a wind storm with a small rudder. He compares the bit and the rudder to the tongue. James uses these examples to illustrate the power of the tongue. He says that controlled speech is a measure of spiritual maturity. A mature Christian is an individual who takes his words and controls them so that the words work for him and not against him. Many Christians have words working against them because they don't listen to what they say. They don't have a clue.

Every time you speak something, ask yourself, "Is that what I want?" James says that by controlling your tongue you control your destiny. You can change and determine the course of your life with the words of your own mouth.

9
CHAPTER

The Law of Obedience

*For as many as are led by the Spirit of God,
these are sons of God.*
Romans 8:14

The Law of Obedience involves yielding to the guidance and the leadership of the Holy Spirit. If you are born again, the Holy Spirit lives inside of you. He was sent to teach you and guide you into all truth. In the last chapter, I showed the connection between what you say and your financial and material well-being. In this chapter, I will illustrate the connection between your financial and material well-being and your submission to the Spirit's leading in your life.

YIELDING TO THE HOLY SPIRIT

Why is this law so important? Why is yielding to the leadership and guidance of the Holy Spirit so important? There are two primary reasons. The first is found in Isaiah 1:19:

If you are willing and obedient, you shall eat the good of the land.

Obedience is the key to prosperity and success in the Kingdom of God. It pays to obey God. I know some readers may expect something deeper and heavier, but this is it: It really does pay to obey God.

Look at Isaiah 48:17:

Thus says the Lord, your Redeemer, the Holy One of Israel: "I am the Lord your God, who teaches you to profit, who leads you by the way you should go."

The Bible says that God will lead you by the way that you should go, not drive you or push you, but lead you. Leadership, however, implies *following.* God is leading, but you have to follow. Demons drive and push, but God leads. Notice, He says, "I'll teach you to profit."

Look at verse 18:

"Oh, that you had heeded My commandments! Then your peace would have been like a river, and your righteousness like the waves of the sea."

Here is the formula for guidance: Profit + peace + righteousness = God's guidance. The word "profit" means to ascend, to set forward, to increase. When God leads you, you ascend, go forward, and increase. When God increases you, He is going to give you peace. Some Christians are getting increase, but no peace, and they are puzzled. They don't have peace because they are out of position. When you get out of position, you are never going to have the peace of God.

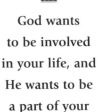

God wants to be involved in your life, and He wants to be a part of your decision-making.

Verse 17 reads *profit*, then verse 18 reads *peace* and *righteousness*, which is right living, virtue, and integrity. God will never guide you in such a way that you have to compromise your integrity. When God guides you to make a deal or to make a move, you can sleep at night. The Holy Spirit lives on the inside of you. He wants to help you succeed in life, if you will learn to listen to Him.

Jeremiah 7:23 says:

"But this is what I commanded them, saying, 'Obey My voice, and I will be your God, and you shall be My people. And walk in all the ways that I have commanded you, that it may be well with you.'"

God says that if you obey Him, if you listen to His voice, it will be well with you. The word "well" means to be happy and successful. Do you want to be happy and successful? Obey God and you will be.

Jeremiah 7:24 says:

"Yet they did not obey or incline their ear, but followed the dictates of their evil hearts, and went backward and not forward."

You were not created to go backward. You don't have a reverse gear. God created you to go forward. It's natural to go forward, but it's unnatural to walk backwards. The Bible says if you don't obey God you are going to go backward and not forward. So, if you are going backward, you need to do a self-inspection because it pays to obey God.

The second reason why yielding to the leadership and guidance of the Holy Spirit is so important is found in Psalm 32:8-10:

"I will instruct you and teach you in the way you should go; I will guide you with My eye. Do not be like the horse or like the mule, which have no understanding, which must be harnessed with bit and bridle, else they will not come near you. Many sorrows shall be to the wicked ["wicked" in this context refers to those who fail to yield to the instructions and guidance of the Spirit of God]; *but he who trusts in the Lord, mercy shall surround him."*

God's vision is better than your vision. For example, when you're driving and you approach a hill, you generally slow down because you cannot see what's on the other side. However, God has the capacity to see both sides of the hill at the same time. He says, *I will guide you with My eye.* God's eyesight (His vision) is far better than our eyesight. I am talking about being led by the Holy Spirit. He is not only on the outside, but He lives on the inside of you as well.

God wants to be involved in your life, and He wants to be a part of your decision-making. Proverbs 3:5-6 says:

Trust in the Lord with all your heart, and lean not on your own understanding; in all your ways acknowledge Him, and He shall direct your paths.

Remember, not everyone will understand what you are doing when the Spirit of God leads you. At times, you won't understand either. That's why the Bible says, *Trust in the Lord with all your heart.* Then it says, *In all your ways acknowledge Him, and He shall direct your paths.* This includes your financial and material well-being: tithing, spending, borrowing, lending, selling, investing, business ventures, choosing jobs, and changing jobs. Before every financial transaction, you should acknowledge God, even when you're considering giving money to loved ones and friends. You should acknowledge God in *all* of your ways.

Now, if that's true, you should never be led by money — even when choosing a job. The job may pay an excellent salary, and it may be a great opportunity for advancement, but how does the job impact your spiritual life and your family life? How do you know this job is a blessing from the Lord? Have you asked Him? In all your ways acknowledge God, and He will direct your paths. He wants to be involved in your life.

HOW THE HOLY SPIRIT LEADS YOU TO PROSPERITY

We have discovered why yielding to the leadership and guidance of the Holy Spirit is so important. Now let's discuss how the Holy Spirit leads you to prosperity.

God speaks to you in many ways. It is important that you understand how to recognize His leading:

He speaks to you through the written Word of God (2 Timothy 3:16-17). All other forms of guidance must line up with the Bible. Isaiah 8:20 says, *If they do not speak according to this word, it is because there is no light in them.* God is never going to guide you outside of His Word. Whenever He guides you, it will be consistent with Scripture.

He speaks to you through creation (Romans 1:19-20).

He speaks to you through the ministry gifts — the apostles, prophets, evangelists, pastors, and teachers (Ephesians 4:11-12).

He speaks to you through other Christians (Romans 15:14).

On rare occasions, He might speak to you through an audible voice. (See Exodus 3:4.) However, don't try to limit God. It is not your prerogative which way He chooses to speak to you. God takes the initiative. When you start asking God to speak in a certain way, you open yourself up to deception. The Bible says that there are many voices in the world and not all of them are God's voice.

He speaks through angels (Acts 8:26).

He speaks through the gifts of the Spirit (Acts 13:1-4). Whenever God uses a prophet or someone to speak a prophetic utterance to you, it should confirm what God has already placed in your spirit. You shouldn't run out and do something just because someone says, "Thus says the Lord." That includes your pastor. If God hasn't said anything to you first, just put this revelation on the shelf, pray about it, and go on with your business.

He speaks through visions (Acts 9:10-16). God speaks through dreams, or what the Bible calls night visions (Matthew 2:13-14; Acts 16:9-10).

There are three major ways that God speaks to us:

The voice of the Holy Spirit (Acts 10:19-20). When the Spirit of God speaks to you, it is very definite, detailed, and authoritative. You will know that God is talking to you. It is so clear that it sounds as if it is coming from the outside. However, the Holy Spirit lives in you and He speaks to your spirit from the inside.

> You can always know the right choice because the Spirit will always bear witness with the truth.

The voice of the human spirit. This is also called your conscience. You'll find references in Romans 2:14-15 and Romans 9:1. In the Old Testament the voice of the human spirit is called the still, small voice. (See 1 Kings 19:12.)

The inward witness. The number one way that God normally speaks to Christians is not by words that we hear, but by an inward witness. Are you born again? How do you know? Okay, the Word says you are, but how do you really know? You know because of an inward witness, an inward assurance, or an inward peace. That's also how you will know when God is guiding you in other areas.

Most of the time when God guides you, He doesn't speak audibly. Most of the time, it is not with a voice. It is just something on the inside that says, "This is correct." That's how God will lead you to find a church or to buy a house or a car. That's how He will show you whom to marry or which job to take or turn down. It is the same inward assurance. You just have to remember to look on the inside. When you first learn to be led by the Spirit, you will make some mistakes, but He will train you and teach you. You have to learn to *trust in the Lord with all your heart, and lean not on your own understanding* (Proverbs 3:5).

There are times when God leads me and it doesn't make any sense to my mind. But I can't listen to my mind; I have to listen to my spirit. When you are about to make a major purchase, like a house, everything can look good, but if something on the inside of you isn't at peace, you'd better pause. You know that feeling, that "something-just-isn't-right" feeling. Pause and pay attention to that warning. If you are looking at a possible spouse but you get that something-just-isn't-right feeling, don't let the good looks and flattering words fool you. You can always know the right choice because the Spirit will always bear witness with the truth. No one should be able to cheat, fool, or swindle you because your inward witness will keep you from these traps.

Notice Romans 8:14:

For as many as are led by the Spirit of God, these are sons of God.

You aren't to be led by emotions. You aren't to be led by feelings. You aren't to be led by your mind. You are to be led by the Spirit of God.

Verse 16 says:

The Spirit Himself bears witness with our spirit. . . .

The traditional *King James Version* says, *The Spirit itself,* but that is not correct. The *New King James Version* says correctly "Himself." The Holy Spirit is not an "it." The Holy Spirit is a "He." He bears witness with your spirit.

Add to that Colossians 3:15:

And let the peace of God rule in your hearts. . . .

This verse is talking about the human spirit as well. There is a witness in your spirit concerning everything. Look in your spirit before you make a decision. When it is time for you to proceed, you are going to have a comfortable feeling in your spirit. Down on the inside you will have peace, an inward assurance, or conviction. When you shouldn't proceed, you will have a sense of uneasiness, a feeling of discomfort. If you don't feel good about it, don't go against that inner prompting, for it is the Holy Spirit saying to your spirit, "Don't do it." However, the Holy Spirit is a gentleman, so He is not going to knock you down to prevent you from doing it. There won't be any lightning bolts or audible voices. God is not going to speak primarily to your body (ears). He is a Spirit, and He will speak to your spirit.

Much of the time the Holy Spirit is not leading people. Instead, they may be led by their own prejudices. I'm not just talking about racial prejudice. People have certain prejudices, preferences, or tastes, and they often struggle getting past them. Many people are often led by their emotions. It is possible to miss God because you are listening to your mind and not to your spirit.

FULL OBEDIENCE TO RECEIVE GOD'S BEST

I had two men tell me years ago that God told them Faith Chapel Christian Center (where I am the pastor) was their church. Yet, neither one of those men attend Faith Chapel. If the Spirit of God told them that, and they did not obey, how are they prospering wherever they are now? Who knows? Maybe what I had to say was the connection to their miracle or prosperity, but they are somewhere else. I doubt that they are walking in a significant degree of prosperity because they chose to be disobedient.

I don't believe you can ignore or neglect God's direction and still prosper. What has God been telling you?

Has He said anything to you that you are not doing? If He told you to do something and you are in disobedience, you cannot expect to prosper.

Let's consider 1 Kings 17:2-6:

Then the word of the Lord came to him [Elijah], *saying, "Get away from here and turn eastward, and hide by the Brook Cherith, which flows into the Jordan. And it will be that you shall drink from the brook, and I have commanded the ravens to feed you there." So he went and did according to the word of the Lord, for he went and stayed by the Brook Cherith, which flows into the Jordan. The ravens brought him bread and meat in the morning, and bread and meat in the evening; and he drank from the brook.*

Because Elijah went to the place called "there," the ravens took good care of him. If he had gone westward or if he had gone to the Jordan River itself and not to the brook, he would have been hungry. The ravens were commanded to take the food to the place called "there." God has made provision for your life, but it is only in the place of obedience and not just anywhere you want it to be. God's provision for your life is in the place called "there." *"There" represents the place of obedience.*

People frequently tell me, "I know I need to be at *your* church, but I am involved in so many activities at *another* church." They make statements like that and then they pray for God to supply all of their need. How can He do that when they are in disobedience?

Look at Acts 16:6-7:

Now when they had gone through Phrygia and the region of Galatia, they were forbidden by the Holy Spirit to preach the word in Asia. After they had come to Mysia, they tried to go into Bithynia, but the Spirit did not permit them.

The Holy Spirit told them not to preach in two different places. We don't know why, but He said, "Don't go!"

Verses 9 and 10 state:

And a vision appeared to Paul in the night. A man of Macedonia stood and pleaded with him, saying, "Come over to Macedonia and help us." Now after he had seen the vision, immediately we sought to go to Macedonia. . . .

The rest of the story is well known, of course. He went to Macedonia and established a church at Philippi.

Now look at Philippians 4:15-18:

Now you Philippians know also that in the beginning of the gospel, when I departed from Macedonia, no church shared with me concerning giving and receiving but you only. For even in Thessalonica you sent aid once and again for my necessities. Not that I seek the gift, but I seek the fruit that abounds to your account. Indeed I have all and abound. I am full, having received from Epaphroditus the things sent from you. . . .

Paul was moving in the direction of Asia when the Spirit of God sent him another way. He received a vision to go to Macedonia and obeyed — being led by the Holy Spirit — and established a church. That church ended up being his financial partner. In fact, that church supported him more than any other church. God knew where the money was and where Paul needed to be. Paul had to obey the Spirit of God, which was orchestrating circumstances, people, places, things, and situations at the right time so that his needs would be met. What if he had gone into Asia? His needs would not have been met, and people would have said, "The Lord is testing you." But his needs would not have been met because of his disobedience.

What has the Lord said to you? Where has He told you to go? What has He told you to say? What are you not doing, where are you not going, or what are you not saying? If you can think of anything, you'd better go back to that point. Your prosperity is related to your obedience. You can't say "no" to the Holy Spirit and expect God to prosper you. Even if you are tithing or giving, if you are being disobedient, you will not fully experience His blessings. Your provision is in the place called "there" — the place of obedience.

10
CHAPTER

The Law of Love

And though I bestow all my goods to feed the poor, and though I give my body to be burned, but have not love, it profits me nothing.
1 Corinthians 13:3

Now that I have covered the first four laws, let's look at the fifth law — the Law of Love, which has to do with relationships. I am reminded of something the Lord said in 1 John 4:20:

If someone says, "I love God," and hates his brother, he is a liar. . . .

Likewise, God asks this question: "How can you love Me, whom you cannot see, and refuse to love your brother, someone you can see?" God equates your love toward Him with your love for others. You cannot separate the two; they go together.

Galatians 5:6 says:

For in Jesus Christ neither circumcision nor uncircumcision avails anything, but faith working through love.

Faith is the vehicle that brings God into your circumstances.

Faith is the switch that releases the power of God. Faith is the vehicle that brings God into your circumstances. In fact, the Bible says without faith it is impossible to please God. (See Hebrews 11:6.) And according to Galatians, faith works by love. So, what is faith? Faith is stepping out and acting on God's Word. Faith is acting out the Law of Renewal, the Law of Giving and Receiving, the Law of Words, the Law of Obedience, and the Law of Growth and Progression.

CONSISTENCY IN YOUR LOVE WALK

Faith works by love, not by itself, which leads us to the first spiritual truth: **The laws that govern riches in the Kingdom of God will not work apart from a consistent love walk.** The Bible connects prosperity to the love walk. When I say prosperity, I'm talking about every realm of existence — spiritual prosperity, mental prosperity, physical prosperity, social prosperity, and financial prosperity.

For example, the Law of Giving and Receiving represents a key component to prosperity in the Kingdom of God. This law does not operate in a vacuum. Regardless of what you are doing in terms of giving, your failure to relate properly to others will undermine the return on your giving.

To prove this truth from Scripture, let's look at Luke 6:38. You really can't teach prosperity without teaching Luke 6:38. However, since the Law of Giving and Receiving does not operate in a vacuum, we must begin with Luke 6:35:

> *"But love your enemies, do good, and lend, hoping for nothing in return; and your reward will be great, and you will be sons of the Most High. . . ."*

Notice how this verse tells you to love your enemies. This involves reacting properly to others regardless of how they may act. God does not hold you responsible for what others do, but He does hold you responsible for your actions and reactions. You cannot control how others relate to you, whether they are kind and speak well of you. You can't stop a man from cursing you, and God is not holding you responsible for that. But God is holding you responsible for your actions, and for how you respond to the ugliness of others.

Notice what it says in the latter part of verse 35 and in verse 36:

> *"For he is kind to the unthankful and evil. Therefore be merciful, just as your Father also is merciful."*

Mercy involves not giving people what they deserve. If they deserve to be cursed out, you choose not to curse them. That's what mercy is.

Now notice what it says in verse 37:

"Judge not, and you shall not be judged. Condemn not, and you shall not be condemned. . . ."

God directs you not to judge and condemn people and not to be a critical person. Don't be a faultfinder — someone who always sees something negative.

Let's turn now to the latter part of verse 37:

"Forgive, and you will be forgiven."

There will be times when people are offensive, but God says that the right response is to forgive them. You don't have a right to hold grudges. God does not give you that right. No matter what they say or what they do, you don't have a right to hold on to the offense. The Bible says your response should always be to forgive. You really have no option but to love people. Other people's wrongs don't give you the right to be wrong, as well.

God says to react properly toward your enemies — to do good, be kind, be merciful, don't judge, and don't condemn. He tells you to forgive in verse 37, and then in verse 38, He tells you to give.

"Give, and it will be given to you: good measure, pressed down, shaken together, and running over will be put into your bosom. For with the same measure that you use, it will be measured back to you."

In connection with all these things, He points out that your giving will work for you. Most people, however, want to start at verse 38 and neglect what the Bible has to say before that.

How you relate to others is important to God.

Some people sit in church holding grudges against a person in the next pew. There are people in church they won't talk to, and yet they are wonder-

ing why their giving is not working for them. It will never work because the Bible connects prosperity to the love walk. The principle of seedtime and harvest is connected to how you relate to people.

I was raised to be respectful. If there is any credit due to someone for this, it goes to my mother and my father because they raised me to be respectful to everyone, not just to them. Perhaps because of that background, the revelation that my prosperity was connected to how I related to people came to me early in life. I latched on to the revelation that my prosperity, my dreams, my hopes, and my desires are connected to how I relate to people. Therefore, I choose to relate well to them.

Initially, I walked in love, maybe somewhat selfishly because I was not going to let anyone cut off my blessings. But as I began to mature in the things of God and my walk with the Lord, I came to find that loving people was easier than holding grudges. It's easy for me to forgive people. I say, "Father, I forgive them, and I release them in Jesus' name." For me, it is easier to do that than to walk around with a load of grievances or resentments.

IMPROPER RELATING WILL HINDER YOUR PRAYERS

Some people are tithing and giving and still wondering why they are not prospering, but the reason is that they are not relating properly to people.

First Corinthians 13 is the great love chapter. Let's look at verse 3:

And though I bestow all my goods to feed the poor, and though I give my body to be burned [This is the epitome of giving. He talks about giving to the poor, and then he says, I go to the top of the ladder and give my life. You can't give any more than that], *but have not love, it profits me nothing.*

Here is what you have to understand: The scripture does not say it would not profit the person or organization you give to. You can hate your neighbor and give me $1,000 and that money is going to be spent the same way. As far as I'm concerned, whether you like your neighbor or not is irrelevant and immaterial because the $1,000 gift will still benefit me. However, it won't profit *you.* If love is not in your heart, your giving won't profit you. It will profit the church, it will profit the poor, it will profit the pastor, but it won't profit you.

How you relate to others is important to God. I'm talking about all of your relationships, not just the people you like. I'm talking about marital relationships, parental relationships, and sibling relationships, as well as relationships in your church, your neighborhood, and your workplace. The way you relate to friends, coworkers, supervisors, subordinates; the way you relate to instructors, teachers, classmates, and administrators; the way you relate to each other in church as brothers and sisters in Christ; and the way you relate to people in the community are all very important to God.

The laws that govern riches in the Kingdom of God will not work apart from a consistent love walk.

You cannot curse your boss and expect God to prosper you. Some people believe for great amounts of prosperity, but it isn't going to happen apart from a commitment to walk in love.

Now let's look at 1 Peter 3:7:

Husbands, likewise, dwell with them [your wife] *with understanding, giving honor to the wife, as to the weaker vessel, and as being heirs together of the grace of life that your prayers may not be hindered.*

Husbands, there is a right way to talk to your wife, and, wives, there is a right way to talk to your husband, even when the other person is wrong. Think about it — how in the world can you prosper if your prayers are hindered? In this verse, God is not talking about your positive confessions of faith, your tithing, or your work ethic. He is talking about how you relate to your spouse, and a failure to relate properly to one another will hinder your prayers.

Verses 8-9 continue:

Finally, all of you be of one mind [be in agreement], *having compassion for one another* [that's mercy]; *love as brothers, be tenderhearted, be courteous* [be kind, don't be rude, don't be ugly]; *not returning evil for evil or reviling for reviling* [that's insult for insult, abuse for abuse, faultfinding for faultfinding], *but on the contrary blessing, knowing that you were called to this, that you may inherit a blessing.*

In effect, God is saying, "If you want a blessing, be a blessing."

Now read 1 Peter 3:10:

For "he who would love life and see good days, let him refrain his tongue from evil, and his lips from speaking deceit."

Some people are gossipers, backbiters, whisperers, and slanderers; they're always talking about other people. Such people are not going to profit. The Bible says if you want to see good days, you have to control your mouth.

Notice 1 Peter 3:11-12:

"Let him turn away from evil and do good; let him seek peace and pursue it. For the eyes of the Lord are on the righteous [the righteous are those who are relating properly to each other], *and His ears are open to their prayers* [not everybody's prayers, but

their prayers]; *but the face of the Lord is against those who do evil."*

God is saying, "I won't hear you if you are not relating properly." He says, "You can pray all day, but your prayers won't get answered." In summary, I hope you understand this first spiritual truth. The laws that govern riches in the Kingdom of God will not work apart from a consistent love walk.

SIN WILL STOP YOUR PROSPERITY

Now, here is my second spiritual truth: **Sin will hinder the prosperity of God from manifesting in your life.**

The proof text for this is found in Proverbs 28:13:

He who covers his sins will not prosper, but whoever confesses and forsakes them will have mercy.

Sin will stop your prosperity. However, many Christians are operating in deception because they have not understood (or maybe they have not been taught) that there are two categories of sin. Most Christians wouldn't dare fornicate. Oh, how disgusting that would be to them! Homosexuality, lesbianism — again, disgusting! They wouldn't drink, smoke, or do anything like that.

But there is another class of sin mentioned in 2 Corinthians 7:1:

*Therefore, having these promises, beloved, let us cleanse ourselves from all filthiness of the flesh and **spirit**, perfecting holiness in the fear of God.*

Many times Christians concentrate on the sins of the flesh (fornication, adultery, homosexuality, drinking, carousing, pornography, gambling, cursing), but the Bible says that we also have to cleanse ourselves from **sins of the spirit.** Both categories of sin will open the door for Satan to come in and steal your prosperity.

Look at Luke 15:11-12:

Then He said: "A certain man had two sons. And the younger of them said to his father, 'Father, give me the portion of goods that falls to me.' So he divided to them his livelihood."

He divided to *them* his livelihood. He gave to *both* sons. The Bible says that the younger son went to a far country and wasted his substance with riotous living — sins of the flesh. He engaged in wild partying and lost everything he had, ending up in the "hog pen of life." Sins of the flesh will cause you to lose what God has given you; **sins of the spirit** will hinder God's prosperity from ever manifesting in your life. The other son didn't live an outwardly bad life. He was a churchgoer. Look at verses 25-30:

"Now his older son was in the field. And as he came and drew near to the house, he heard music and dancing. So he called one of the servants and asked what these things meant. And he said unto him, 'Your brother has come, and because he has received him safe and sound, your father has killed the fatted calf.' But he was angry and would not go in. Therefore his father came out and pleaded with him. So he answered and said to his father, 'Lo, these many years I have been serving you; I never transgressed your commandment at any time [a self-righteous, holier-than-thou attitude]; *and yet you never gave me a young goat, that I might make merry with my friends* [jealousy]. *But as soon as this son of yours came, who has devoured your livelihood with harlots, you killed the fatted calf for him.'"*

The oldest son was filled with bitterness, resentment, and an unforgiving spirit. Notice that he says, "This son of yours," which implies, "He is not *my* brother anymore; he is *your* son. I'm through with him and I have cut him loose." Is there anyone you have "cut loose"? Do you have a narrow-minded attitude or a haughty air that seems to declare that you are better than others? That is religious bigotry. Some Christians are filled with hatred and prejudice. Are you prejudiced? Are you a gossiper, backbiter, slanderer, or whisperer? Are you mean, rude, or unkind toward others?

Someone might respond, "Well, that is just my personality. That's just the way I am. I'm just straightforward."

No, if you're the type of person who has a nasty, rude personality, then you need to change because God didn't create you that way.

Look at verse 31:

"And he said to him, 'Son, you are always with me, and all that I have is yours.'"

The older son appeared to be doing everything right, but his attitude was holding him back. Sins of the spirit are more dangerous than sins of the flesh because they can lay dormant for years. The older son said, *Lo, these many years.* . . . You can harbor unforgiveness and resentment for years without understanding the negative results of these sins.

If you are doing everything else right, yet still not prospering, you should check this area of your life. You will never prosper until you make some changes. You can choose to have a nasty attitude, harbor grudges, and operate in resentment, but you are also choosing to forfeit your own prosperity.

11

The Law of Growth and Progression

Cast your bread upon the waters,
for you will find it after many days.
Ecclesiastes 11:1

I believe the Law of Growth and Progression is the balancing law, the law that keeps us from falling into the ditch on either side of the road. Let's define these two terms. "Growth" implies development, and it means to increase or to expand gradually; to develop little by little. The word "progression" means to move forward or to move onward. It means to continue to develop by successive steps. If, for example, I wanted to walk up the steps to a stage, I would stand on the first step, then stand on the second step, then stand on the third step, etc., to get to the top. That is successive, progressive, step-by-step movement.

As this law relates to the Christian experience, and specifically to prosperity, it is important to do likewise — first, stand on the bottom and take one step after another until arriving at the top. To take one step and go to the top is not natural. If you enter an elevator on the first floor, you don't push a button and in a blink find yourself on the twenty-fifth floor. No, you have to pass twenty-three other floors, and then you arrive on the twenty-fifth floor. In light of these examples, here is my first statement of truth.

The Law of Growth and Progression is an all-inclusive prevailing principle of the Kingdom of God. This law covers everything. Now I will give you some illustrations or examples of what I am talking about.

First Peter 2:2 states:

As newborn babes, desire the pure milk of the word, that you may grow thereby.

This verse is talking about spiritual growth and development. It is talking about spiritual maturity, which the Bible says is developed by stages. Here, the Scripture talks about a spiritual babe in Christ, but Ephesians 4:14 talks about the childhood stage of spiritual development. Then Hebrews 5:14 talks about the adulthood stage, implying that you don't get saved today and become fully mature tomorrow. So, this Law of Growth and Progression involves time and patience. It takes time to grow up.

Second Peter 3:18 commands God's people to *grow in the grace and knowledge of our Lord. . . ."* You don't learn the Bible overnight, but you can grow in grace and grow in knowledge over a period of time.

Second Thessalonians 1:3 encourages God's people to grow and increase in love. As you mature spiritually, people won't upset you as much as they once did. You won't get offended as quickly, and you won't have a chip on your shoulder. As you mature in the things of God, you will find it easier to respond in forgiveness.

Second Thessalonians 1:3 also teaches that you can grow in faith. Faith is a like a muscle which can be developed. I remember years ago when we at Faith Chapel Christian Center believed for $5,000 each Sunday in tithes and offerings. It took every bit of the faith we had to believe for that $5,000, but today our church is believing for millions of dollars for our building projects. When we were a young ministry, God never would have given us million-dollar assignments because we hadn't developed our "faith muscles." We just weren't ready.

Finally, Romans 8:28-29 talks about being conformed to the image of Jesus. God's ultimate purpose is that each believer be conformed to the image of Jesus. Second Corinthians 3:18 says that we are changed into His image from glory to glory. Fulfilling God's purpose doesn't happen overnight. Can you see that the Law of Growth and Progression in the Kingdom of God covers everything?

PROSPERITY IS NOT AN EVENT — IT'S A PROCESS!

Now, let's go to our second statement of truth.

Prosperity in the Kingdom of God is not an event. It is not instantaneous — it doesn't happen overnight. Let's put it like this: God doesn't pay off every Friday. We are talking about lifestyle Christianity. In the Kingdom of God you are not going to prosper overnight.

Notice what Exodus 23:20 has to say:

"Behold, I send an Angel before you to keep you in the way and to bring you into the place which I have prepared."

> If you hang in there with the Word, God will turn your life around.

God told Israel that He would send an angel, and that angel's assignment was to cause them to prosper and enter into the promised land — the land of milk and honey. I believe the angels still work to cause Christians to prosper in the Kingdom of God.

Notice Exodus 23:28-29:

"And I will send hornets before you, which shall drive out the Hivite, the Canaanite, and the Hittite from before you. I will not drive them out from before you in one year, lest the land become desolate and the beasts of the field become too numerous for you."

It took time for Israel to overcome their physical enemies, and it will take time for you to overcome your financial challenges. Success will not happen overnight.

Now notice verse 30:

"Little by little I will drive them out from before you, until you have increased, and you inherit the land."

How does prosperity come? It happens gradually by increments, "little by little" until you have increased and you have inherited the land.

Again, prosperity in the Kingdom of God is not an event. It is not instantaneous. It is important for you to understand this point. If you don't, you will start to expect everything to happen yesterday. When it doesn't come to pass that quickly, you may become discouraged and want to throw the Bible away and say the teaching on prosperity does not work. Well, let me tell you it does work!

Now, here is a scripture that many readers can quote by heart, but how I'm going to interpret this scripture may disappoint or surprise you.

Look at Ecclesiastes 11:1:

Cast your bread upon the waters, for you will find it after many days.

You'll find it after many days — not tomorrow, not next week. The definition of the word "many" is abundance or an abundance of days, after a long time. You are not going to give a one-time offering and all of a sudden your problems will be gone. It's going to take time. It took years for you to get in the hole you are in, and it's going to take some time to get out of it. If you hang in there with the Word, God will get you out of it and turn your life around.

I am talking about a lifestyle, not an event. In Scripture there is a difference between a miracle and a harvest. Oftentimes believers emphasize miracles. The Bible is full of the miraculous. But for Christians, the emphasis is on harvest because we don't have a promise of a miracle in the Word of God. I would like a miracle. I want someone to give me $20 million tomorrow so we can finish our Family Activity Center and go on to the next phase. We should expect and desire the miraculous, but we don't have a scripture to believe for a miracle. We do, however, have scripture to believe for a harvest.

There is also a difference between a miracle and a harvest in terms of time. Miracles are instantaneous; there is no delay for the most part. But in a harvest, it takes time for the seed to develop and grow. There is also a difference between a miracle and a harvest in terms of the initiator. God by His Spirit initiates miracles. First Corinthians 12:11 says that the Spirit manifests Himself as He wills, but the Bible teaches that a man can initiate a harvest.

It's important to know that lifestyle Christianity is not a quick fix, which leads me to my third statement.

The desire for fast money and the temptation of quick prosperity are of the world, and they lead to bad decision-making, compromise, and poverty.

We make a mistake when we promise people something quick. It is not going to be one offering you give, or just one decision you make that is going to change your life. That microwave or express-line concept is not of God. The Bible actually says the opposite. Don't just accept what people say at face value. Just because a man or woman of God is on television doesn't mean everything they're saying is right. Just because somebody writes a book, or dresses nice, or lives in a nice house doesn't mean his or her theology is right. The Bible says in Acts 17:11 that the Bereans searched the Scriptures daily to see whether or not what Paul and Barnabas had said was true. That is what we are supposed to do as well.

Now look at Proverbs 19:2:

Also it is not good for a soul to be without knowledge, and he sins who hastens with his feet.

The word "hasten" means to be speedy and quick, in a hurry. Notice, the scripture says to *be without knowledge.* It is not good to be ignorant. The *New International Version* of the Bible says, *It is not good to have zeal without knowledge, nor to be hasty and miss the way.* When you are in a hurry you are going to miss the way.

My prayer life and my walk with the Lord have been established over a period of years. My giving has been established and developed over a period of years. In fact, Faith Chapel Christian Center has been established over a period of years.

Proverbs 20:21 says:

An inheritance gained hastily at the beginning will not be blessed at the end.

The Bible says you can acquire wealth quickly in the beginning, but in the end it won't be blessed.

Next, read Proverbs 21:5:

The plans of the diligent lead surely to plenty, but those of everyone who is hasty, surely to poverty [or lack].

You are going to love this one. See, these laws work, but they don't work overnight. We go out and mess our lives up, get ourselves into all kinds of financial bondage, and then we want to come to church and in one day get our lives back together. We say, "We're giving you three weeks, Lord, to get this thing together!" But we spent the last ten years tearing it up. Remember, your credit doesn't become bad overnight.

Look at what Proverbs 28:20 has to say:

A faithful man will abound with blessings, but he who hastens to be rich will not go unpunished [or the *King James Version* says *"innocent."*]

The word "innocent," as it is used here, means to be blameless, to have integrity. There is a contrast here between a person with a get-rich-quick mentality and a person who is diligent and consistent, someone who is in the Word, giving and living upright week after week, month after month, year after year. That is a faithful person, someone who is consistent, steadfast, and constant. The Bible says that such an individual will abound with blessings.

In fact, one translation says that a person who attempts to get wealth quickly will end up compromising and making bad decisions.

Listen to what God has to say in Proverbs 28:22:

A man with an evil eye hastens after riches, and does not consider that poverty will come upon him.

Don't allow yourself to get caught up in the enticement of quick success to the point that you will compromise godly standards. You might as well settle in and say, "I'm going to do this for the rest of my life. I'm going to live this way." And you might as well say, "I'm going to be a giver for the rest of my life." I know some people say they'll be glad when the church's building project is over, but after it's finished there will be another one. God is always doing something, and He will always challenge you to give. This is part of the Christian lifestyle.

God's best is manifested through the Law of Growth and Progression.

GOD WANTS YOU TO HAVE HIS BEST!

God's best is manifested through the Law of Growth and Progression.

Let's look at Luke 15:22:

"But the father said to his servants, 'Bring out the best robe. . . .'"

The father in this story is representative of our Father God. I believe it is the will of God for His children to enjoy the very best that this life has to offer — the best housing, the best clothing, the best transportation, the best education, the best recreation, or whatever. Here is why I believe this: I believe God is a Father. He is a real "Daddy," and I believe He epitomizes what I'm supposed to be as a father. I want the very best for my two children. I don't want them to struggle, and I don't want them to start off where I started. I want them to be far beyond where I started. I want them to live in the best houses, drive the best cars, wear the best clothes, and have plenty of money. However, God's best is manifested through the Law of Growth and Progression.

I get this concept from Mark 4:26-28:

And he said, "The kingdom of God is as if a man should scatter seed on the ground, and should sleep by night and rise by day, and the seed should sprout and grow, he himself does not know how. [This is why I say men initiate the harvest — it says, "If a man should scatter," not "If God scatters." God initiates miracles, but a man must scatter seed on the ground. Now look at what happens.] *For the earth yields crops by itself: first the blade, then the head, after that the full grain in the head."*

Isn't that progression? "First the blade, then the head [or ear], then the full grain [or corn] in the head [or ear]." You won't get into trouble if you follow God's order.

Some people struggle because they are not following His progression. They are trying to have the full corn in the ear when they are at the blade stage. I take what God is saying to mean that every level should be better. I should go from a starter house to a better house, and keep going until I get into God's best. If I drive an automobile, the next one should be better, and the next one after that should be better still, and offer more options.

Even in my giving, the next year I should give more, and so forth, until I end up in God's best. So, the only pressure I have is what I put on myself, not what some preacher puts on me. The only pressure is to get better and better.

Unfortunately, many people don't do that. They may understand the first part — that God wants them to have the very best — and then they go out and get into a house and can't pay the mortgage. If you're in a house and can't pay the note, God didn't give you that house. You probably needed to go from your apartment to a starter house, and then go from the starter house to a better one. You keep moving up, and the next thing you know you are in a really nice community. Before long you are standing in the Promised Land.

Some people try to jump from their old car to a Jaguar or a Mercedes. God wants you to have the Jaguar, but you have to purchase more than just the car. You've got to get the insurance, and that's going to cost more than that Pinto you're presently driving.

Then there's maintenance. When you take that Jaguar in for service, it's going to cost you plenty. But some people stretch to get that big, nice car and can't afford the insurance or the regular service the car requires. It's just a machine; it's just metal, and it needs to be serviced. So, the car begins to fall apart, leaking oil and running badly because they couldn't afford the regular mainte-nance. They should have bought a car that didn't cost so much, but they couldn't take their eyes off that Jaguar.

Then there are the designer clothes. Men who can't pay their bills are trying to wear alligator shoes. Some ladies buy $500 or $600 hats. If they got a cheaper hat, they could probably get more than one. No matter how nice that hat looks, after wearing it about eight times in a row, people will say, "Oh, Lord, here comes that hat again."

Some Christians are financially impulsive. They're out far beyond where their faith is, so they may have to use wisdom and turn some of those high-priced cars back in. They made those purchases on their own and then said, "God blessed me." Now they are struggling with those high-priced items. Do you think God is going to jump out there and help them? He is not obligated to pay their notes if they didn't talk to Him first. If we would listen to the Spirit of God, we would find that He's very practical. The Holy Spirit will lead you progressively. (On the other hand, some people are still in the blade stage when they should be further along.)

Now, it's going to be a little embarrassing to take things back, but don't worry about what people say. They aren't paying any bills for you. Get yourself at a place where you can get some of that pressure off, where you can start exercising your faith, and when God starts moving you up, you can pay your bills and move up some more.

Some people in the church appear to be prospering when they aren't even tithing. I don't care what kind of house they're living in or what kind of clothes they wear. If they are not tithing, they are not prospering according to God's standard.

GROWTH REQUIRES TIME AND PATIENCE
᪥

Growth implies time and necessitates patience.

The very fact that it is a growing process implies that it is going to take time. If you plant a seed in the ground, it is going to take time to grow, sprout, and mature.

Look at Hebrews 6:10-15:

> *For God is not unjust to forget your work and labor of love which you have shown toward His name, in that you have ministered to the saints, and do minister. And we desire that each one of you show the same diligence to the full assurance of hope until the end, that you do not become sluggish, but imitate those who through faith and patience inherit the promises. For when God made a promise to Abraham, because He could swear by no one greater, He swore by Himself, saying, "Surely blessing I will bless you, and multiplying I will multiply you." And so, after he had patiently endured, he obtained the promise.*

Don't compare your prosperity with anyone else's because you don't know what kind of giving they have been doing, or what kind of confessions they have been making. You don't know how long they have been walking with the Lord. You don't know what battles they have come through, and how long they have been faithful to God. If you have recently started applying these laws of prosperity, you can't compare yourself to someone who has been doing this for years. The Bible

> You have
> a right to
> expect to live
> a supernatural
> and
> prosperous life.

says that Abraham obtained the promises through faith and patience. You must be patient also.

God is not only concerned about your financial prosperity; He wants you to develop character and spiritual maturity. Most of us have unresolved issues in our lives. It takes time to push out all the junk we've accumulated through the years. God cannot afford to put a whole lot of money in some people's hands because in some cases it would devour them. God moves on a different timetable, which might seem slow to some, but He has to prepare us for prosperity. However, the fact that He takes the time to prepare us for prosperity and patiently guides us progressively forward indicates His desire for us to have total life prosperity and not just financial abundance.

The Scripture says in 3 John 2:

Beloved, I pray that you may prosper in all things and be in health. . . .

I hope that I have been able to show you how much God loves you, how much He desires for you to live a first-class lifestyle, and how He wants you to be in a position to finance the evangelism of the world. You may be one of the countless Christians who thought that "rich" was a bad word. However, nothing could be further from the truth. Not only does God want you to be rich, He wants that wealth to be acquired by methods that will not destroy your family relationships, endanger your health, or sabotage your relationship with Him.

On a regular basis, review the six laws that govern riches. Remember, they are laws or principles that work the same every time, in the same way, for everyone. Because God is no respecter of persons, if you embrace these truths and conduct your life by these godly principles, you have a right to expect to live a supernatural and prosperous life.

May you be richly blessed, may you richly bless others, and may you be used by God to advance His Kingdom.

Prayer of Salvation

God your word says in Romans 10:9-10 that if I confess with my mouth the Lord Jesus and believe in my heart that God raised Jesus from the dead, I would be saved. I repent of my sin and I now confess with my mouth and believe in my heart that God raised Jesus from the dead and that He is Lord. Therefore, I make Jesus Lord of my life. I repent of my sins. I now call you Father God. Thank you for forgiving me. I am a new creature in Christ Jesus. I am born again. I am in the family of God.

SCRIPTURE REFERENCES:
Romans 10:9-10
II Corinthians 5:17-18

About the Author

Michael D. Moore was a student at Samford University's Cumberland School of Law when he was called into the ministry, and in 1981, with four people and a Bible, he began Faith Chapel Christian Center in the den of his home. From this humble beginning, the church moved progressively from Dr. Moore's home to a funeral parlor, to the YWCA, to an abandoned school building.

Faith Chapel Christian Center is now approaching a nondenominational membership of over 6,000 and is located on 140 acres of land in Birmingham, Alabama, where the previously abandoned school building now serves as the Administrative Offices for this continuously expanding ministry. In 2002, Faith Chapel Christian Center completed construction on a 3,000-seat, $15 million dome sanctuary — built *debt-free* — while the church assisted other ministries with liquidating their own debts.

The church is currently involved in another debt-free building project: Phase II of the City of Deliverance, which will eventually include five major centers of ministry (the Activities Center, the Center of Ministry, the Business District, the Education and Development Center, and the Health Clinic).

Dr. Moore has a prophetic teaching ministry, which is founded on the simple yet profound truth that "the Word of God is the Answer." His immense popularity is a result of communicating this message on a practical, applicable level, which inspires and empowers people to live successfully and victoriously on a spiritual, physical, mental, social, and financial level.

The ministry's major outreach tool, "The Word of God is the Answer" television program, airs in several cities throughout the United States.

Dr. Moore has also written two life-changing books on financial prosperity: *God's Heavenly Banking System,* and *What a Difference a Dime Makes.*

Dr. Moore is married to Kennetha Moore, who oversees the Children's Ministry, the Women's Ministry, and the Bookstore. The Moore's have one son, Michael, and one daughter, Tiffany.

Other Books by Dr. Michael D. Moore

God's Heavenly Banking System

Tithing: What a Difference a Dime Makes

Cassette and CD Series by Dr. Michael D. Moore

Success Conference 2006

If Loving You is Wrong, I Don't Want to Be Right
(Singles Fellowship)

Weep Not: Overcoming Grief, Disappointment and Loss
(2 volumes)

God's Will is Healing

Did You Fail or Are You a Failure?

Diligence (3 volumes: Start/Continue/Finish)

Fruitful Life

Faith: The Currency of Heaven

Enemies to Peace: Depression/Discouragement/Suicide

Confidence: The Pathway to Peak Performance and
Recognition

Lord, Do Me a Favor

For further information contact:

Mike Moore Ministries
866-236-WORD (9673)

www.MikeMooreMinistries.org